The Lost Name: A Novelette

Madeleine Vinton Dahlgren

THE LOST NAME

A NOVELETTE

BY

MADELEINE VINTON DAHLGREN

AUTHOR OF "A WASHINGTON WINTER," "SOUTH-SEA SKETCHES,"
"SOUTH-MOUNTAIN MAGIC," "MEMOIR OF
ADMIRAL DAHLGREN," ETC., ETC.

BOSTON
TICKNOR AND COMPANY
1886

𝔘𝔫𝔦𝔳𝔢𝔯𝔰𝔦𝔱𝔶 ℜ𝔯𝔢𝔰𝔰:
JOHN WILSON AND SON, CAMBRIDGE.

PREFACE.

ALTHOUGH this little book claims on its title-page to be a " novelette," some portions of it have perhaps the improbability of romance. Nevertheless, its plot is in part woven out of facts connected with the devastation wrought by the French Revolution of the last century, through which a family that emigrated to America lost its name. Moreover, the characters portrayed are not in every instance pure idealizations.

M. V. D.

SOUTH MOUNTAIN HOUSE,
March, 1886.

(RECAP)

CONTENTS.

———◆———

THE LOST NAME.

CHAPTER I.

MY GRANDFATHER'S SECRET.

THERE are losses — and there are losses! and each and every loss involves privation. Mankind deplore the ravages of fire, of water, of all elemental strife; they bewail the deprivation of fortune, and bereavements by death; they waste the fleeting moments of Time, and have often to endure loss of health: but the want that threatened to make a tangled riddle of my life was the most perplexing of all mysteries, for it was caused by the effacement of *a name.*

Can thought exist without expression, or individuality become distinctive without being defined? Yet in such a bewildering situation was I involved, and in such a network of intangible resistance was I enshrouded. I was a victim swathed in an imperceptible net which was fine spun as is the spider's web, yet grasped me so firmly in its invisible tenure that, struggle as I would, I could not free myself.

In a certain sense the course of every man's life is more or less of a labyrinthine maze, and multitudes grope out their feeble lives and aimlessly fall into graves whose head-stones indicate them more clearly than the under-laid dead ever succeeded in defining themselves when living, inasmuch as there, at least, they have found a habitation and a name.

.   .   .   .   .   .

My earliest recollections are of the dear, aged paternal grandfather, who after the untimely death of my parents remained sole surviving guardian of my youth.

I had in infancy a little sister, Estelle, whose sudden taking away gave me the first ineffaceable impression of death.

I was but a baby of four years of age at the time, but the scene painted itself from the visual retina deep into my infantile brain, and has ever remained to my inner perception a clear and transparent image.

The wee one had, some weeks previous, it seems, one day awakened sooner than was her wont from her noonday sleep, and impatient to free herself, had, in trying to climb over the sides of her crib, fallen to the floor. Her screams called to her aid the careless nurse, who hushed her quickly to a renewed slumber; and the accident was forgotten, only to be recalled some weeks later, when the injured infant was suddenly seized with the convulsions of

death. The impressionable baby brain had
at the time of the fall received a fatal jar
that soon developed this mortal malady.   I
was passionately fond of my little sister, and I
tried to rouse her from her drooping drow-
siness into a romp with me and engage
her in a mimic battle. We were thus at
play in the nursery, an imaginary king
and queen, striking at each other with
some thin bamboo reeds which our nurse
intended to sew into her calash, when Estelle held her tiny hand to her drooping
head and began to moan.

Thinking at first that she meant surren-
der, I shouted with all a boy's loud vehemence, "*I* am the king, and *you* are nothing!" waving my reed in triumph; but in
another moment, with a twitching movement
and glazed eyes, she tottered over into my
arms. Ah, the dismal tragedy enacted that
night! During all its continuance no one

noticed me, and I took note of everything,
— my poor grandfather's groans, the busy
feet of the terrified servants hurrying to
and fro, the dazed dismay of our wretched
nurse, the solemn gravity of the doctors
who were called in consultation; but above
all our hapless darling, so rigid and stiff
in the intervals of her convulsive tremors.
And at last my horror culminated when a
swollen vein in the neck was opened, and
slowly the drops of congested blood oozed
out. Then whiteness, stillness, hardness,
rigor, death.

Sooner or later, few mortals escape the
vision of a death-bed scene. My infantile
eyes had now beheld this awful mystery. I
was as yet a baby in years, but I was never-
more to be like other children in childish
glee.

The old homestead had rested in deep
shadow before; but my little sister and I

had dwelt in our own sunshine and not understood how heavily the atmosphere around us was freighted with woe. We had been all unconscious that our gifted father and lovely mother were no more, and that the silvered locks and furrowed brow of our beloved grandfather betokened heart-break as well as length of years.

But now my aged parent alone remained, and I began to realize that he was dejected and spiritless, and that we lived in a dull, drowsy, moping way.

Thus it was that I grew into a sort of abnormal existence, as a nervous, sensitive youth with acute perceptions made morbid by the manner of my bringing up. But on one point in particular the natural vivacity of youth seemed to add to, rather than diminish, and that was a sensibility that had become almost a disease. As I grew older, the shade of the upas that saddened and depressed me only increased its malign in-fluence. My interest in the world around me diminished; and at a period when my eager thoughts would naturally have been occupied with that future which every young person so longs to grasp, I rather shrank back into myself.

I was the victim of a mystery I sought in vain to penetrate.

.   .   .   .   .   .

My grandfather was a French *émigré*, and he had fled from France in 1793.

He never wearied telling me, and I never wearied listening, to the recital of the dreadful scenes he had witnessed in Paris during those appalling days of wrath and judgment heaped upon an afflicted people. Finally, he had fled horror-stricken from the tempest-tossed city.

Coming to America, he had at first sought the kindly aid of several gentlemen

who were friends of his family at home;
and later on, a career of honor, wealth,
and usefulness had been his.

Then calamity came; his wife, his only
child my father, and my mother, whom he
had loved as a daughter, had all died.
"Ernest, we are now all alone," was often
the sad ending of a story. But more often
he would in an obscure way, which concealed more than it revealed, hint darkly
at some family secret which was to be confided to me only when I should reach more
mature years, — "years of discretion," as he
would phrase it.

To a child of my peculiar temperament
this mode of procedure was most harassing.
This untold secret weighed so heavily upon
my imagination that it early in life became
a constant subject of my speculations.

My grandfather was an insatiate reader,
and would sit for hours reclining in his

chaise-longue in the quaint old library, poring over some favorite author, while I would study every line and wrinkle of the aged face as if I were a seer to compel by some process of divination the occult to make itself manifest. But the countenance I sought to interpret, like a warped mirror, failed to give forth a true image of that which I desired.

Then, again, the construction of the old homestead was so very odd and unusual as to enhance any fanciful impressions I might have. It was a large, rambling mansion, which had been purchased by my grandfather half a century previous, and added to by him from time to time, without any attempt to produce a homogeneous effect. The exterior aspect was as a result very confusing, but the interior arrangement was simply bewildering. There was a succession of nooks and crannies, dark closets and galleries,

narrow passages that like blind alleys led no-
where, but perchance terminating in a blank
wall.   The chiefest charm of the irregular
old house to me, however, was its rude, unfin-
ished garret, dimly lighted with little high
dormer-windows which were filled in with
minute diamond-shaped panes and arched at
top.   Through these narrow apertures the
rays of the sun faintly glinted and fell in
checkered patches upon the dark oaken
floor, or exposed the lair of the fierce, hungry
spider, whose ensnaring web festooned the
place.

" Has he too," thought I, " a secret, that
he ever lies in wait, springing swiftly out of
dingy corners at unexpected moments, and
then anew spinning mazy folds of entangle-
ment ? "

I felt sure that he was a magician pun-
ished for some misdeed, so marvellous was
this intricacy of his network, and thus

doomed to toil on and plot sanguinary meshes to entrap the unwary.

The very entrance to this curious loft captivated me, as one climbed up a very narrow dark stairway that hugged the wall at the end of a long narrow room. This apartment was used for all the various purposes of housekeeping, and my grandfather, who had a fancy of naming each distinctive portion of his house, called it " The Nondescript." This appellative suited well the varied uses for which this room was kept. It had a sweet odor of the dried herbs that hung suspended from its rafters, and its numerous closets were the special pride of our old Annette.

I dearly loved when a boy to climb the steep stairway that led directly into the loft I have described, and wistfully peer around, examining with eager interest the massive chests that were ranged like portraits of stately ancestors in rows.

2

My father had been a sea-captain and had wandered far and wide. He led a restless life filled with gallant deeds; but he had a passion for roaming, and my grandfather once had told me that he was ever in search of something that he had never found. At last, scarcely having reached life's meridian, he came home to die of a fever. Had his mantle of restless endeavor fallen upon me?

How attractive were those iron-girt chests of his! Oh, if only I could unlock their clasps, perchance I might find the clue to the family secret!

Then there were dainty and odorous boxes of camphor-wood brought by my father to my mother from China, and now filled with all of earth's vanities that had ever appertained to her. These were the only fresh pleasing objects in the musty garret, and I used to sit upon them and wonder if mamma saw her lonely child. Or, had *they* the secret? I once had heard my grandfather tell Annette that " women could worm out *any* secret; " and mamma had been a very clever woman, I was told.

One day, being about twelve years old, as I sat moping in a corner of the loft, musing in a dreamy way very unusual for a boy, my quick ear caught the sound of the hesitating steps of my grandfather ascending the creaking old stairs. I sat very still, because I was half afraid of being found there, and so I was not noticed. He came slowly enough, shuffling along, but at last he stood still near the entrance of the loft.

After a few moments' pause he groped his way to one of the sea-chests, and stood so very near me that he must have seen me, had not his frame of mind been so concentered. There he stood, beside this expressive memento of his dead, the very picture of woe.

Stretching forth his senile hand, he cried out: " My son, my son, child of an ill-fated sire, thou hast fallen into a nameless grave."

And here, overcome by his emotion, he sank down upon one of those grim sea-chests I had so often longed to examine, in the hope to find therein my secret. After an interval of sighs and tears, he feebly arose and tottered out of sight.

Those words, "fallen into a nameless grave," sounded always in my ears. Were they in any way connected with that secret I so longed to know?

Then, how often did I hold silent colloquy with the old house, appealing to the walls that sheltered me to declare their record! But no responsive echo answered back.

Once, indeed, my heart beat high, for I felt sure that I had at last discovered the ever-elusive mystery. It was perhaps a year later than the scene in the garret, and I was one day restlessly pacing my room, when I perceived a very slight vibration under my feet, always at the same place. I paused, and made sure that there was a perceptible trembling when I pressed heavily on the spot.

I then removed the heavy carpet that prevented a closer scrutiny, when I again discovered a slight oscillation at the same place, which upon being pressed, yielded, and a small trap-door opened. A deftly contrived hiding-place was thus disclosed between the floor and the ceiling below.

I was at the moment overjoyed; but, alas! upon a careful examination there was nothing but an enclosed empty space. Once again I was disappointed, for *there* was no secret. Yet it was such a neatly contrived place of concealment that my curiosity was aroused, and I determined to mention the circumstance to my grandfather. He smiled and said: " Ernest, you gave yourself much trouble to no purpose. Formerly there was no bank in the adjacent town, and I brought a carpenter from a distant city to construct this trap-door and the enclosed box, as a place of deposit for my valuables. At present my papers of consequence are kept in a fire-proof safe at the bank. I had forgotten all about this trap-door; but, like its master, it must be getting rickety with age, else you could never have noticed any giving way at the joints."

Encouraged by his communicative mood, I ventured to confess frankly to something of the emotions that had so long filled my heart regarding the family secret he had more than once hinted to me existed, and disclosed to him that I was always anxiously seeking to solve the riddle. I ended by saying: "In fact, dear grandfather, I can bear anything better than this dreadful uncertainty."

He smiled for a moment, but almost at the instant looked very grave and dejected. He was at that time over eighty years of age, and I, an impulsive youth scarcely in my teens. It seems impossible for children to realize the feebleness of age, or measure with their thoughts that the flickering light readily goes out. It rather appeared to me, that the life he had so long borne would wear on like a smouldering flame that lasts indefinitely. So not understanding that there was for him an open grave into which any slight deviation might readily precipitate him, I heeded his words but little.

There was a pause, and I can now recall that he motioned to me very quietly to come nearer, pointing at the same time to a footstool upon which his slippered feet rested. I sat down beside him.

"Ernest, my child," he murmured, "be not over eager to know that which is better unknown, neither strive after the unknowable."

Here he heaved a deep sigh and gazed at me with immense pity, as if with a prophetic eye he could divine my future. But when I felt sure that he was about to satisfy my great desire, he remained silent; and soon after, with trembling steps, he sought his bedroom.

I brooded over his few mysterious words, "the unknown — the unknowable." I was but a lad, and of an impressionable temperament. Difficulties only aroused my natural ardor; and with the eagerness of youth and the sublime assurance that ignorance engenders, I determined to conquer "the unknown."

But "the unknowable!" Here I paused as on the threshold of a dark abyss. Time wore on, but rather increased this fever of the imagination.

At sixteen, one becomes impatient of all restraint, and I was bent upon forcing my grandfather to give up his secret. I fancied continued suspense impossible.

One sultry summer's evening we two sat together in the gloaming. There are days in every year which, like battles, are dangerous to human life, but especially hazardous to that existence whose silvered thread hangs by the frailest tenure. The thermometer was high up in the nineties and the heated air gave forth no life. My grandfather reclined with closed eyes in his *chaise-longue.*

I had been taciturn and moody for some time past; and selfishly wrapt in my own thoughts, had not observed his increased despondency and declining strength. In old age childhood in many ways repeats itself, and the octogenarian needs light, cheerfulness, and constant care.

How often, later on, these reflections embittered me with vain regret! How often could I have wished that this last sunset had been irradiated with brightness and the glow of devoted affection!

I had resolved to insist upon an explanation of the mystery that harassed me, on the very first suitable occasion, and it seemed to me that the present moment was most opportune. My grandfather was not occupied in any way, and I could claim his attention.

So, seating myself beside him, I said: "Grandfather, pardon me if I am unreasonable, but I beg you once more to confide to me everything concerning my family history. You cannot, my dear sir, imagine how much suffering this mystery has cost me."

There was a slight twitching of the eyelids as he muttered, " Ernest !" then there was an interval of silence. I felt as if I could not endure it; and hastily rising, exclaimed : " This is torture, sir ! I cannot, I will not, bear this suspense. Kill me, or tell me the secret."

" Tell you and kill you, simpleton," mumbled he.

" Yes," cried I, " let me know all; what care I for consequences ? "

" And has the hour come ?" groaned he, feebly. " Yes, I feel the life-current ebb low. Come closer, lad — it is dark — in thine ear — only one word — one little blank word; " and with a gurgling, painful effort he hissed, " *nameless.*"

" *Nameless !* " shouted I, losing all self-control, " what child's play is this ? Why nameless? In what way nameless? What nameless deed?" And I angrily strode the apartment. Never before had I so far forgotten myself in the honored presence of one whom I loved most tenderly. But the storm of long-repressed passion overmastered me, and tossed by the whirlwind of my own emotions, I was oblivious to all else.

The cyclone passed, and I paused. The venerable head had sunk upon his bosom, the arms hung listless at his side. There was a something of utter abandonment in this attitude that startled me and recalled me to a sense of my misconduct. I hastened to support the bent form. He was — dead!

"Accursed secret!" shouted I, "fiend-like, thou hast stripped me of all peace, and now thou snatchest away the only life to which mine is bound! No, rather," I cried, "accursed curiosity, thus to deprive me, by my own crime, of a life I should have cherished!"

I knelt beside him and lovingly pressed his cold hands, I bathed them with my tears; and as I thus bent over his rigid frame, the servants hurriedly entered, brought thither by my cry of distress.

CHAPTER II.

MY COLLEGE DAYS.

M Y grandfather had not made a will, and
as I was his sole heir, the court pro-
vided me a suitable guardian. The only
trust that he left, was a letter addressed to
the president of the bank where his strong-
box was deposited, requesting that a certain
package therein placed should not be opened
until I was of legal age, and it was then to
be handed to me intact. It was conjectured
that this package contained valuables, although I felt quite certain that it would inform me of the family secret. Yet, what an
interminable period of time to wait! At sixteen, five years appears an endless duration;

but at eighty, doubtless it must have seemed but a brief limit. And thus I remained at the homestead, after this deep affliction, for the space of a fortnight very sad, quiet, and inert.

The great and to me sudden change was difficult for a youth to grasp. I had fallen into morbid ruts of thought; and still remaining in the same house, even the severe ordeal through which I had passed had not shaken me out of the grooves in which my days were set. But happily boys are not allowed, as girls often are, to mope out an existence, nor is it expected that they will sit in the shadow of closed doors and darkened rooms when death claims their dear ones. Nor are they heavily draped in suffocating crape, that throws a dismal pall over all nature, whenever they do emerge from a gloomy house. But, on the contrary, boys are expected to restrain their emotions and grapple almost at once with the exacting duties that must fill their time.

Evidently my guardian so thought. He was a man of sturdy honesty of purpose, and had been selected by the honorable judge on account of his high character as a business man to guard the interests of a youth who was entirely alone in the world. He measured all events by the rule of three, and never conceded the least infinitesimal fraction in his calculations to sentiment of any kind. In fact he took an absolutely unimpassioned view of every matter that came within the scope of his care or observation. This straightforward manner certainly made his judgment very valuable, because it was based upon the most undeviating rectitude. His quality of being a safe adviser had procured him in the community such great confidence and respect that he was a sort of residuary legatee for all the estates to be

settled, a protector of all the orphans whom
the providence of God had left with moneyed
interests to be looked after, and the confidential and true friend of all the widows who
were in danger of being robbed. Dear Mr.
King, truly did he bear his right royal name!
Had he flourished as a Roman citizen, this
epithet would have been bestowed upon him
as an agnomen well merited. And so, as
to fidelity, honesty, and unselfish devotion,
virtue was replete in him; but as to sensibility, sentiment, or idealism, he was but a
man of wood.

With the perfect system he always brought
to bear upon the affairs that commanded
his attention, he had within a fortnight after
my dear grandfather's death not only admin-
istered upon his estate, as far as could be
done in that short time, but he had also
made all the necessary arrangements for my
education during my minority. I was sent

to a college where I should receive an excellent classical education and also meet young men who would be suitable companions and even friends for me in after life. Mr. King argued in my case, that, as I was to inherit a considerable fortune, it was essential that I should be well drilled in the classics, as the sure foundation of polite acquirements. " A gentleman of means," he said to me, "must acquire a love of literature and an acquaintance with the best processes of thought. In this way he must inevitably form a high standard, and he will be saved from those low vices that endanger alike health and reputation. Business methods will also, it is hoped," he added, " be evolved out of the mental discipline one must undergo."

My grandfather had died in the last days of August, and I was entered two weeks later at the precise day upon which the new annual course began. My alma mater was richly endowed and one of the oldest educational institutions of the country. What an immense change in all my modes of thought and action! Upon being duly examined as to my proficiency in various branches, I was entered as a freshman.

I had previously been well instructed by masters whom my grandfather had carefully chosen, who came at stated times and gave me private lessons. I studied well enough; but without any special inducements to succeed, not much progress was made. Two things were against me, — I lacked emulation, and I had an undue self-conceit; but these are the ordinary pitfalls to be dreaded by wealthy young men who are taught at home by private tutors.

At the period of which I write, few of our best institutions of learning included in their curriculum any studies appertaining to the domain of physics or of technics, for the wonders of the natural sciences and the mechanic arts were made to yield to the claims of the classics. Nor were athletic sports then considered as of 'much consequence. But a considerable proficiency in mathematics, a built-up system of ethics, and the most arduous and unceasing drilling in the classics, made the principal standard of what was required. Such a course of study was well suited to the natural bent of my inclinations; and having grown up without young companions and with sedate habits of thought, I was soon recognized as one of the close students of the college. My preference also placed me with a certain set of young men who, like myself, were really in earnest to acquire knowledge, although my reticent moods deprived me for a long time of any particular friend.

My considerate guardian had arranged
that I should have the undisturbed occu-
pancy of my room, and agreed to meet
the increased expense thereby incurred.
Indeed he confessed to me, that he had
in his early college days suffered tortures
from having to endure the tyrannous freaks
of a room-mate who never studied if he
could help it, and was principally bent upon
having what he called "a good time," which
consisted in a series of plots to annoy his
preceptors if possible, or certainly his comrades. After having endured at the hands
of this young savage various unpleasant
surprises, such as only college boys can
invent, he finally succeeded in making an
amicable compromise with his tormentor, to
the effect that whenever he was left undisturbed by him, he would prepare the themes
of his room-mate in addition to his own.
This was too advantageous an offer to be

rejected, and gained the student the quiet possession of their room.

This disagreeable experience of my guardian had doubtless led to his stipulating that I was to be left alone, — a privilege that exactly suited my temperament, and was highly appreciated by me. Most people, young and old, dread solitude; but in so doing they do not fully measure the terrible suffering which the constant presence of others inflicts. To a person of acute sensibility, or to one of a reflective disposition, seclusion at certain intervals of time is an absolute necessity. It has often struck me, that the most distressing trial of poverty, one more difficult to endure than cold or hunger, must be experienced in an enforced gregarious manner of living. Oh, the ineffable horror of being hopelessly condemned to live amid a seething mass of humanity!

I once knew a charming old gentleman who had risen to the highest grade of the diplomatic career and was an immense social favorite. He was suave, affable, and most companionable. He entertained with graceful ease and was an ornament to society. Yet he had never married. But he was so invariably cheerful, and even debonair, that one could not suspect any disappointment of the affections ever to have darkened his life. It was, to say the least, odd that he had chosen to remain single. At last the riddle was solved; for one day being in an unusually communicative mood as we two puffed away at our post-prandial cigars, he broke in upon that delicious silence, which only those who understand each other can enjoy, with the remark, —

"Have you any idea, Ernest, why I never married?"

"Not the remotest conception, my dear sir," I answered, with unaffected surprise.

"I am the victim of an idiosyncrasy," said he, rather mournfully. "You find me reaching into the autumnal shadows a solitary man, because it has ever been a necessity of my nature to remain absolutely alone from time to time. There are periods, oft recurring, and occasionally lasting for days at a time, when I feel compelled to seek communion with myself and retire from the pressure of the material cares that surround me, to the contemplation of those subjects that can only be considered from within the fortress of one's own inner consciousness. It may be a dual self that demands audience; but from whatever source the exaction comes, it is peremptory."

My astonishment as I heard these words, uttered with so much feeling, was extreme, and I could scarcely realize that it was the whilom gay diplomat who had spoken; for as I regarded him as he momentarily paused in his recital, I seemed to look upon another manner of man. There was a prescient look in his deep-set eyes that reached out into vague depths far beyond the transparent atmosphere with which I had hitherto seen him surrounded. But the abstraction was evanescent; for almost at the instant recovering himself, he added cheerily, —

" The androsphinx has spoken, and you may well see why he remains isolated."

" The promethean fire of love was needed to irradiate," I replied.

" You are all too young," he responded, " even to appreciate the divine privilege of solitude. Yet you can at least understand, my dear fellow, why a wife would have too seriously infringed upon these chosen periods, dedicated to so supreme a pleasure. In fact I could not have asked another to share my life, and then claim exemption from her companionship. Even were she so good-natured as to overlook my eccentricities and pleasantly receive me when I should anew seek her presence, I should in the meantime reproach myself, and all the more so because she was such an angel of goodness."

Again he paused, as if the pleasing image of so great and amiable forbearance was an alluring temptation; but almost at the instant added with energy, —

"You see, Ernest, exactly how it is that I could never marry, no, never."

.　　.　　.　　.　　.　　.　　.

Well, however it may be as regards a matrimonial alliance, one thing is certain, — that, sooner or later, a chum is indispensable to a collegiate. Intimacies I never contracted, but of friends I was happy to possess two: we three were chums. Three boys more unlike each other could scarcely have been found than Herbert Shirley, Claude Bonac, and myself. All paradoxes found their exemplification in us, for we agreed to disagree, and out of the diversity of our natures came unity. And even in marriage, I am told, dissimilarities make the most perfect unions; that is, if these diversities are governed by a law of accord, — as, for instance, the complete blending a skilful artist produces in the use of contrasts. He has seized the key by which Nature unfolds to him the uses of her seven colors, through whose tints she diversifies the landscape with an infinite variety of beauty. It requires a certain compass of notes to produce harmony, and in man alone we find the wondrous diapason full. Nothing wearies like sameness, for variety is a fundamental law of nature. So in both love and friendship, if strong individuality does not exist, life drags fearfully amid the dreary waste of monotony. It is dissonance, not diversity, that produces repulsion.

Claude Bonac was, like myself, of French

origin, and our Gaulish blood asserted itself. Probably of all nationalities the
French make the most indifferent emi-
grants; for they never entirely dissociate
themselves from the parent stem or ingraft
on another stock, inasmuch as they always
think of themselves as exiles from home,
and in their inmost thoughts live French
scions still.

It must have grown out of some unde-
veloped affinity of this kind that we became friends, for Claude was my very
opposite as to disposition. He was as
facile as I was reserved, as loquacious as I
was taciturn, as companionable as I was
shy. But we were both alike eager in the
acquisition of knowledge; and although
Claude's mind was not so receptive as my
own, yet he was of more ready apprehen-
sion. In our debating society, where we
wrestled for honors, the vivacity of his

speech made him a dangerous opponent.
I admired him greatly, and I may candidly
say so without the least admixture of envy
on account of his being the fortunate pos-
sessor of so much that was denied to me;
while Claude honestly confessed that I held
a real influence over him.

It is true I admired Claude, but I loved
Herbert Shirley. Dear Herbert, glorious
youth, born to climb, and with ever sure
and steady ascent place still higher an honored name! Shirley was of direct descent
from titled English ancestry; but he held
any inherited distinction simply as a sacred
pledge confided to him as an earnest of
high endeavor. He was thus also true to
his more precious birthright as an American. He was rather exceedingly winning
than handsome, although of fair proportions and manly bearing. His mind was
clear and expansive, but he was chiefly

remarkable for the universality of his gifts. He had that most comprehensive of all faculties, — the poetic gift; and he was also an artist, handling the palette with consummate taste, and setting his colors so as to mirror nature true and fair. He produced charming pictures, that had not only force of coloring and great freedom of treatment, but often also infinite tenderness and sweetness of expression. Herbert likewise excelled in athletic sports, and was an authority on these subjects among his comrades. Strange to say, he loved study too, and competed for the honors of his class. I esteemed him for all these traits, but I loved him with an affection exceeding that I had ever before entertained, because he was so high-minded, so unselfish, and so entirely free from egotism.

As we steadily worked our way up from class to class, I led the ranks as the most laborious student, and Claude brushed against me shoulder to shoulder as we struggled up the steep ascent, leaving Herbert third. But I always recognized that Shirley might readily have been fair and square above us all, had he brought just a trifle more of energy into his achievements. The very comprehensiveness of his talents worked him a disadvantage. The facility with which he gained success caused him perhaps to undervalue its advantages. And yet he had splendid *verve* and dash. It is a pleasing consolation to linger over the fair picture after this interval of time; for alas! the ardent sun of this bright life, which so rapidly hastened to scale its meridian height, soon sank to its decline. But an untimely death could not obscure a memory ever fresh in the hearts of those who knew him only to love him.

Commencement Day, closing the third

year of my collegiate course, brought to my labors the most ample recognition; and it was with heart elate that I stood upon a raised platform, in presence of an applauding audience, to receive the first honors of my class. Yet even at that moment of fruition I experienced, like a flitting shadow, a half regret that Herbert did not share them with me. Yet he was third, and in everything was mentioned as " distinguished;" and of all present he rejoiced the most that I had won.

Claude, who was second man, did not attempt to conceal his chagrin, although he had the manliness to shake hands and say openly: " Confound it all, just to have missed the top round. But it is fairly yours, Ernest; I would have crowded you back if I could have done so."

One of the real pleasures of the day was the attendance of Mr. King, who had taken the time from his overcrowded engagements, and came to my room to congratulate me when all was over.

"You have well profited by my advice, Ernest," said he; "and I trust, my boy, that these honors are but the harbingers of the world's acclaim."

"Scarcely so, sir," said I; "for I have rather compelled success by hard labor than won it by superior talent."

"Better yet," replied he; "you have found the right royal road. Only persevere!"

"I have that within me, sir," said I, "that forbids me to pause, for I crave knowledge; or at least I am ever devoured with desire to grasp the unknown. I am curious to know more and more."

As I made use of the word "curious," the recollection of the longing to know a certain secret that had once consumed me, came back with force. But the momentary

4

yearning was almost as soon repressed by
the thought that three of the five years had
already melted away like the mists of the
morning.

My guardian must have interpreted my
silence into the wistful desire of youth for
change, as he asked me, —

"Ernest, where would you like to spend
your well-earned rest this coming vacation?
Would you prefer to return to your own
homestead, where Annette and the cobwebs
await you, or to take a reasonable sum of
money and the excitements of a journey?"

I could not but smile at the characteris-
tic word "reasonable." Evidently my guardian was highly gratified, and wished to
permit me some amusement such as I
might select, but was anxious that my rec-
reation should be strictly within the bounds
of reason; and his worldly wisdom taught
him that the surest restraint was in a lim-

ited purse. Some parents and guardians of wealthy young men act in the most sodden-witted manner as regards the future of their charges, supplying them with large amounts of money to spend in a reckless way. They might as well sow dragon's-teeth, to insure a harvest of vices, as thus to throw their gold pieces broadcast in the hands of inexperienced youth.

"I have an invitation, sir," I answered, "which I should much like to accept;" adding with warmth, "for I love the dear fellow."

"Love is a strong word, especially to apply to a man's own sex," replied Mr. King with a smile; "but pray who is your friend?"

"He whom you noticed, Mr. King, and spoke of as being of great promise, — Herbert Shirley, I mean; he ranks only third man of our class this year, but I assure you, sir, in point of absolute talent he stands first. I have an invitation to spend my vacation with him at his homestead."

" Ah, yes! " said my guardian. " The Shirleys, of Shirley Manor; they are an old Maryland family, and have occupied their homestead from the early days of our Colonial history. But, Ernest, I have reason to know that they are poor, very poor. Are you sure that Mrs. Shirley expects you, my lad? "

There was a cold business tone in the concluding words, as if Mr. King were making a mathematical calculation as to the expense the Shirleys might incur on my account, and just a doubt of the advisability of my acceptance.

" Herbert Shirley is not a man to make a mistake, Mr. King," said I, somewhat irritated by the implied doubt in my guardian's manner. " He read me a portion of a letter from his mother, extending a most cordial invitation to me to return with her son. It was written, I assure you, sir, with graceful insistence."

With provoking imperturbability, Mr. King again responded, — "Ah, yes, Miss Darcy, who became Mrs. Shirley, was deservedly a great *belle* in her day, for she was a most accomplished woman, who would be likely to write a charming letter."

"Then you know about the family, sir?" I inquired, rather surprised at my guardian's loquacity, for he was as a rule silent as regards people, being usually very reticent, and speaking only upon topics of general interest.

"Certainly," he responded. "The Darcys were well known as among the oldest families of the Eastern shore. Herbert's mother was an only child who lived with her widowed mother at the place now called Shirley

Manor.   She was a lovely girl, and the toast
of all the gallants the country round; but
she gave no preference to any of her suit-
ors.   But finally, being on a visit to Washington, she met young Shirley at a ball at
the British legation.   He was a younger
son of a good family in England, and had
been sent over to America to see the country.   He was a handsome young man,
courteous and affable.   It was what is
called a love-match, and ended by the
young couple residing with Mrs. Darcy at
the old place, which from thenceforth bore
the name of Shirley Manor.   This selection of a residence was indeed one of the
conditions of the marriage, as it was understood that Clare Darcy was never to
leave her mother.   Indeed young Shirley
was too madly in love to hesitate about
the acceptance of conditions; friends, family, country, all were alike cheerfully given

up for the woman he loved. They were
married, and Shirley was doubtless a happy
man as far as one in his situation could
be. The listless life he led suited his
tastes, for he was essentially a dreamer, and
occupied in writing for various magazines;
but he never understood the management
of the Darcy Farm, and they were not, in a
worldly sense, prosperous. After his marriage he never received the least aid from
his relatives abroad, for they were displeased
that he had left his country to become an
American. Indeed, it is more than prob-
able that they never knew he was in
straitened circumstances, for both he and
Mrs. Shirley were very high spirited. Some
five years ago the poor lady had the misfortune, in the course of the same summer,
to lose both her mother and her husband,
and she was left almost unprovided for,
with two children, a son and daughter.

I had the gratification at that time to extricate the Darcy Estate from some complications that had arisen, when I again met Mrs. Shirley, after an interval of a score of years."

"You know them, then?" I exclaimed, taken completely by surprise.

" To be quite candid with you, Ernest," he replied, " and in a spirit of confidence, an admiration for this interesting lady was the weakness of my youth."

And so, thought I, *who* may hope to escape if this wise man confesses to a weakness? I answered, having mentally applied his case to myself, —

"And Miss Shirley, does she resemble her mother? Herbert tells me that, next to his mother, she is the joy of his life."

I at once felt that I had spoken inadvertently, and was misunderstood; and I blushed, as only a very innocent young man would

blush, — which of course must have deep-
ened the impression Mr. King had evidently
received through my awkwardness, that there
was an added motive for my wishing to
make this visit. Well, perhaps there was, if
I had closely analyzed my feelings. But, as
is usual with the very young and inexperienced in the emotions, I turned aside from
all self-examination, preferring not to scan
myself too closely.

"Be careful, Ernest," said Mr. King very
gravely, "of the vivacity of impressions
that may interrupt study and engross all
your thoughts. It seems to me that a month
at Shirley Manor will be more likely to
interfere with next year's progress than a
season at Saratoga."

"Not so, sir," said I, "your fears are
groundless; and I shall hope to allure you
to look in upon me at my own home after
my return. Perhaps, too, I may induce

Herbert to come back with me, when you
will see for yourself what a splendid fellow
he is."

"Thanks, Ernest, I fear that there is not
much hope of my having the time to spare.
Take good care of yourself, and my com-
pliments to Mrs. Shirley."

CHAPTER III.

SHIRLEY MANOR.

I DID not accompany my friend when he left for home that evening, but told him that I would in a few days do myself the pleasure of accepting his invitation. I was in fact restrained by a sentiment of delicacy, which bade me permit the first outburst of joy upon the family reunion to expend itself unchecked by my presence. Meantime, I amused myself in the inspection of the public buildings at Washington, — an occupation which is interesting to every American, especially to an ardent youth who fancies that he may become a future legislator for his country.

Some days later, I took an evening boat, and the next morning got off at a landing about ten miles distant from Shirley Manor. I had purposely avoided mentioning the precise hour of my coming, so as to spare my hospitable friend any possible trouble in my regard.

The place where I disembarked was appropriately named Mousetown, and was but a straggling hamlet, with the inevitable post-office, grocery, dry-goods, and provision store all in one building. The tavern next door had a well-provided bar-room, and the landlord stood behind a counter in a sort of den where were barrels of whiskey and shelves well filled with bottles of liquor. Closing in this cuddy from the saloon was a stout oaken door that moved up and down in grooves, and could be very quickly clamped down and fastened inside with a strong iron bar, upon the first mutterings of any disturbance that might involve a raid on the liquors. Outside were various store-boxes, and lounging upon these in dreamy repose during the intervals of their drams, were the idlers who frequented the bar-room and who were facetiously dubbed "the store-box brigade." They bore themselves with an air of dogged unconcern that would have done credit to the veterans of any cause.

The people of Mousetown had built their houses as crowded together, each with the doorstep directly on the rough pavement, as if land meant dollars, in place of cents. The entire scene was not inviting. Pigs had rooted for themselves comfortable snoozing-holes in the soft sand, and the neglected children were diligently heaping up piles of dirt-pies not far off. Here and there were little darkies stretched full length on their backs, kicking up their heels against the sun, and bellowing like very Mycetes; for this race, young or old, must forever be making a noise. Although it was a hot summer's day, the windows of these houses were shut tight, and were closed in with green paper-blinds drawn down full length. But each front door opened directly into a room, and was thrown back so as to disclose a full view of the interior,—mothers rocking away, suckling their offspring with bared bosoms and as little concern of the world without as Eve in the Garden of Eden; or glimpses of rocking cradles tended by wee ones not much bigger than the babies within; or women busily engaged in sewing, rocking as fast as the stitches flew: always and everywhere rockers, rocking. If the men were listless in Mousetown, the women, on the contrary, had discovered the secret of perpetual motion. It was all so new to me, so different from the cleanliness

and retiracy of a New England village,
that I lost myself in contemplation, oblivious for the time being of the Mecca I had
in view, or that I had in turn become an
object of intense curiosity to the assembled
denizens of Mousetown, curs, cats, rats, and
mice included. My attention was recalled,
however, by a hard-fisted, red-haired son
of Erin, whose seedy clothes and battered
hat did not diminish the swaggering gait
and jaunty scrape with which he advanced
to meet me.

"An' if it's a convyance yer honer would
be afther, me, Jerry Maloney, is the mon
to give yez an honest lift."

"Yes," I said rather slowly, as I sur-
veyed my Jehu and felt half ashamed of
being driven to the house of my friend
after such a fashion, "yes, I wish to go to
Shirley Manor."

"An' shure it's me charryot 'ill be afther

the bargin, — tin dollars fur tin miles, 'an she's a beauty. Look, mon, she's forninst yez." So saying, he pointed to a rickety open shed near by, where an old rattle-trap stood under cover.

I was not the man to be unequal to the situation, and before another hour we were dragging through the heavy sand, well on our way to Shirley Manor. The dust was so intolerable that, despite the heat, I pulled up the glass of the shaky doors. After we had proceeded some distance, we came upon a fine smooth dirt-road, bordered on either side with overgrown and untrimmed hedges, which had been once carefully planted; and I soon saw evidence of what had been in former days a beautiful place, but was now much neglected and grown wild. Presently we had a full view of a long, low, rambling, one-and-a-half story frame-house, that had a very wide open portico

. with a sloping roof running around it on three sides. This, then, was Shirley Manor.

The house was admirably situated on a little eminence, from which a spacious lawn gracefully inclined, and through which a semicircular carriage-drive led with an easy sweep to the broad steps that ascended to the veranda.

The noisy vehicle had announced itself; and as we came to a sudden and full stop with a jolt, I leaped out to meet my friend, who had bounded down the steps to welcome me. As I slammed the loose door of the carriage after me, I tossed the driver the stipulated sum, and was in the act of making my bow to the two ladies who had advanced to greet me, when a very decided punch in the ribs threw me on my knees at the feet of the lovely Selina Shirley. And thus it was that from the first instant of our meeting I did her homage! But at the same moment

Herbert, who had seen the thrust aimed at
me, but not in time to parry the blow, laid the
irate Irishman flat on his back and sprawling.

The scene was really too ridiculous, and
I could not at the instant divine what the
cause of offence had been. But as Jerry
sprang to his feet, shaking his doubled-up
fist, he ripped out a profusion of " begor-
ras," " be Jabers," and other elegant exple-
tives, while at the same time he pointed to
the broken window of his vehicle. I comprehended that I must have caused the mis-
chief when I made my too-sudden exit into
the arms of my friend.

" I 've a notion to kill the fellow ! " cried
Herbert, infuriated at this insult to his guest
on his very doorstep.

" Don't touch him, Herbert ! " I said ; " not
until I have paid him. Don't you see that
I unwittingly did the man a wrong when I
broke the windows of his Noah's ark ? "

The ladies had precipitately retired, when I handed Jerry Maloney another ten-dollar note, and at one and the same time gave him a vigorous kick, as I cried out: "Now begone!"

Thereupon the fellow, scrambling up to his driver's seat, shouted as he made off: "Long life ter yer honer! yer a gintlemon every inch o' ye!"

It was certainly a unique introduction to the home of my friend!

Although in our university parlance we called ourselves "men," I was after all but a boy of nineteen, and entirely unused to those gentle influences that make home so endearing; for previous to my college life my days had been solitary and cheerless. The mortifying incident I have related, produced in my breast such a tumult of embarrassment during the meal that was served soon after, that I was scarcely aware of the charming presence of Mrs. Shirley and her captivating daughter. But the finished grace and ease of Mrs. Shirley speedily overcame my confusion; and when, after dinner, I strolled about the pleasant grounds with Herbert and his lovely sister, I was exceedingly happy.

Not far distant from the picturesque old house, with its quaint English chimneys, dormer-windows, and gable-roof, was a restful spot where a drooping willow and a cluster of silver-maples vied with each other in forming an umbrageous arch over the clear surface of a limpid spring. Seeking the repose that this inviting nook offered, we seated ourselves upon a rustic bench; and amid the blending play of light and shadow that surrounded us, we imperceptibly drifted into much confidential talk.

" I am rejoiced," said Herbert, " that you are at last with us, Ernest. It is a pleasure I have so long anticipated."

"And I too," added his sister, "heartily welcome dear Herbert's friend, for I am but a reflection of my brother. So, as he calls me Selina, pray give me the same name. Do not be so formal as to address me as Miss Shirley; that will be proper for others, but not for Herbert's best friend."

These kindly words of friendship, uttered by this beautiful girl, were indeed addressed to me, but the winning glance that accompanied them was entirely given to Herbert. I knew that I was in her eyes only as one favored by him, and the very tone had but one meaning, and that was, "for Herbert's sake." Despite the gracious words, there was an indefinable *hauteur* in her manner that made me half afraid she might take it all back the next moment. So I hastened to say: "If, indeed, anything can add to my happiness in being your brother's friend, it is that I may also be yours, Miss Shirley;

and if I may venture to call you Selina, will you not in turn call me Ernest, as Herbert does ? "

" Certainly," said Herbert, with his infectious laugh ; " that's only fair, Selina, and it completes the introduction so unceremoniously interrupted by Jerry this morning." And so, with the freemasonry of youth, we all laughed heartily.

There was a bubbling of small talk, a fusillade of little things that fell and splashed amid our mirth, as if we had thrown pebbles in the crystal spring that mirrored us so true. Still lingering near this fountain, the slanting shadows of the closing day insensibly inclined us to a more serious mood, for the stillness and tranquillity of the coming eve held us as an absolute influence.

There had been a momentary pause, and Herbert's eyes were taking on that dreamy look that with the poetic temperament often ushers in higher thoughts, when Selina said : " Herbert, have you ever mentioned to Ernest any of the superstitions of Shirley Manor ? "

" No, never, sister mine," he replied ; " the traditions of our dear old home could scarcely find a fitting place for their narration, except within the charmed circle of the Fay's Spring."

" And at the twilight hour," said Selina ; " these are two conditions favorable to us now. Where shall I begin ? Ahem — Sir Knight, once upon a time there was a giant, and — "

" Oh, do not, sister dear," said Herbert, whose mood of dreamy quietude was jarred by the tone of levity.

" Herbert does not like any jesting where our cherished home is concerned," answered Selina; " he loves even all the odd notions of old family servants connected with its sur-

roundings.   And I am glad he does.   Ours
is one of the Colonial homes, and portions of
the house were built over a hundred years
ago ; and what is still more rare in America,
the same family, from father to son, have
occupied the same house all this time.   Of
course we have rooms in which some family
tragedies have occurred; and one in especial,
where, strangely enough, successive members
have, without any selection of the spot, died
upon the same bedstead.   The record of this
room has been so intertwined with our supreme moments, that we have a belief that
the dream of any one who for the first time
is our guest, if he occupy this room and this
bed for the first night spent under our roof-
tree, will be in fact a mirror of the future,
a sort of horoscope drawn of his or her life."

"And very strange things have happened,"
said Herbert.   "Only last year, Ernest, during my summer's vacation, sister and I were

seated in this room one afternoon, looking over some old letters that had been
written by our grandparents, when the door
opened very quietly, and both Selina and
I saw at the same moment that it was held
by a hand which we instantly recognized
to be the precise counterpart of one we
had seen some days before upon a man
who had died a very miserable death. He
had always been very dissolute, and finally
got into a brutal fight, in which he lost a
thumb and little finger, these portions of
his hand having been literally eaten off by
the person with whom he was fighting. He
died of lockjaw, and in great torture of mind
as well. We both saw this mutilated hand
holding the door, and we knew it, as we had
visited the poor fellow on his death-bed."

"Our mother," interrupted Selina, " was so
sure that there must be some one secreted
in the house, whose hand we had seen, that

she had a most diligent search made everywhere."

"Had this been seen by only one of you,"
said I, "or, indeed, had you even been
conversing at the time about the fate of
this poor fellow, this apparition might be supposed to be the effect of a vivid imagination
or of an optical illusion; but under all the
circumstances it was most extraordinary."

"The impression it made upon us both,"
said Herbert, "had all the force and vivid-
ness of a material presence."

"It was awfully uncanny," sighed Selina,
covering her face with her shapely white
hands, as if to shut out a disagreeable object
that had obtruded itself.

An earnest desire to occupy this room
took possession of me, as all the longings
of my life to divine that which existed, but
was hidden, again resumed their sway. Can
it be, thought I, that I have been led to read

my secret in the oneiromancy of this weird spot ?

" Pray, Herbert," I asked, " do me the favor to let me occupy your chamber of divination to-night."

" It is at best but a dismal place," said Selina, " and we had prepared a much more cheerful apartment for your use, Ernest."

" Thanks," said I ; " if you will but humor my caprice to-night, I shall perchance all the more enjoy your kind thought in my behalf, during the rest of my stay at Shirley Manor. It is all like magic here, anyhow," added I, quite unconscious of the peculiar compliment.

Our conversation on the subject was at this moment cut short by the appearance of Mrs Shirley, who joined us, saying, —

" My children, I must remind you that the dews of evening on the Eastern shore in mid-summer are not very conducive to health."

And so we all returned to the house. Tea was served in the library, and we had music, which I greatly enjoyed. Herbert had a fine baritone voice, and accompanied his sister in some duets, while Mrs. Shirley played upon the harp some touching Welsh airs. I could well understand how much she must have been admired when, in the bloom of youth, she had evoked such harmonies as then enchanted my ear. Both mother and daughter were of the same type, — stately women, with mild but dignified manners. Herbert was more winsome, but not less noble. The entire evening was like a glimpse of a new and better world for me, tossed as I had been on a sea of loneliness.

No further conversation had taken place concerning the haunted chamber, and I began to fear that my request would not be granted, when to my gratification Herbert conducted me himself to the apartment.

"I can but hope," said he, "that the fatigues of the day will give you a quiet slumber, Ernest, for I am weak enough rather to dread our superstition."

"I have, as you know, Herbert," said I, "considerable power over my will, and I shall *will* to dream; for I am more curious, perhaps, than even you, old fellow, may imagine."

"Then dream away, and happiness attend you," said he; "only be sure to remember all the visions of the night, so that we may divine your future to-morrow." He closed the door, and I was left alone.

The room was, as Selina had said, rather dismal. It was long and narrow, with a low ceiling and small windows. The carved-wood mantel was high, and had a representation of a band of dancing nymphs bearing garlands of roses upon its face, and the carving was well done. But the wall-paper was dark, and was filled with a confusing medley of statuesque figures, that in the dim light of my candle might readily resolve themselves into illusory, and perchance malevolent, shapes.

But the bed! Its black mahogany stood grim and frowning, the high four posts like sentinels on guard; and the canopy overhead was draped, as were the windows, with Canton cretonne, which in its day, when so few things were brought from China, and at such great expense, must have been deemed rich and rare. The barbaric figures in black, on a chocolate-colored ground and in impossible attitudes, stared at one from the windows or bent mockingly over the bed.

This, then, was the spot where Herbert's ancestors had given up the ghost, where they had dreamed their last dream, then sank into that unconscious slumber that knows no waking. What flitting visions,

what haunting vagaries, might not still in-
fect the air? Life, after all, is the dream,
and death the reality. Here, then, was
fought that last fight between that fleeting
phantasm called Life and that absolutism
called Death. The record of what has tran-
spired must be indexed on these gloomy
walls and imprint itself, like a lingering echo
imprisoned in some vaulted cavern, upon the
slumbers of those who rest here. Yet no,
it is not the Past whose spectral shape con-
fronts one here; Selina said explicitly, that
it was the Future that disclosed itself in this
place by some strange agency.

" Hail, mysterious Future, I invoke thee ! "
I cried, as I disposed myself to sleep upon
the fateful bed.

But my brain had become too excited to
gain the refreshing oblivion I coveted. In
my overheated imagination my past life, with
its undivulged secret, *would* associate itself

with the present situation and with the future of this household. Thus, craving that rest which was so elusive during my struggle with the insomnia that so unexpectedly beset me, the midnight hour was reached. My taper had expended itself, and flickering out, left me in the dark. Finally my eyes closed; but the expectant mind remained alert in all its faculties. Nor did it seem an illusion when suddenly the room was filled with numerous roseate cloudlets massed against a background of permeating light. I was aware that some agency, evolving an element I knew nothing of, was rapidly disposing these vapors into one cohesive form. I also understood that a similar process took place in the act of dissolution, when the spirit becomes subject to new laws, and the soul that is redeemed is separated from the gross clouds of materialism that here below hold it down in sensuous bonds.

But now, having gained the victory through death, and being no longer confined by the prison of the body, it seeks, through uncreated light, the needful power to rise. Animated by this expansive force, it ascends.

These ideas were infused, as I beheld the compacted clouds assume immense proportions, ever following the radiant light, mount higher and higher still, until the apex-point for mortal vision was gained. Thus, like some vast lustre of adoring incense, the soul slowly rises, impelled to seek its primal source, yet faintly, and still more faintly, held back by impurities not fully purged. As I gazed, trembling as to the issue, I saw that light must prevail over darkness; and soon the empyrean opened, and through the rifted clouds I beheld the fluttering soul of my Herbert, freed from shadows, illusions, and conflicts, enter a body, impassible and glorious, and soar aloft.

6

"It is Herbert!" I cried with transport. "Herbert, the immortal youth, behold his pure spirit mount the skies!" In the vague distance countless angel-heads filled the illimitable space, ravishing harmonies floated out through the riven heavens, and above all I could plainly hear through all the circumambient air, clear-toned, trumpet-tongued, exultant, his jubilant hallelujahs!

.   .   .   .   .   .

The scene changed. I felt myself to be sinking, sinking; darkness fell upon me like a heavy veil, so heavy that it was palpable. I knew that my soul, so recently uplifted, was now once more sense-bound. I yearned for wings upon which anew to rise; and the very thought produced a faint crepuscular light, as if I had touched upon some elemental energy, and I realized that the desire to rise corresponds to a hidden power that acts as a motor. Encouraged to know that I was a free agent, I cried out with all the power I could command: " I *will* to see!" when instantly the blackness that had covered my eyes like a pall fell off in scales, and I discerned standing beside the bed a little old woman busily spinning. Then, by an interior illumination, I perceived that the distaff held the thread of my own life. As I marvelled, I felt myself so entangled in the cobweb meshes of its texture that I asked: " Am I a free agent ? " Yes; I had a power of will. Could I disrupt the thread ? Yes; but what next ? Then I started back in solemn dread, as I distinctly heard my grand-father's warning voice pronounce the mystical word " Unknowable !" Thereupon came an oscillating movement, as I was swayed to and fro by some terrible vibratory agency; and as I felt the house to be sinking into some cavernous depth, I was overwhelmed with fear. Amid the destruction of the structure, as all seemed to be breaking up around me, I beheld Selina standing, very pale and erect, within an arched doorway which tottered as if about to crumble. I strove to gain her side and support her, but was held back by the distaff of the spinner, which opposed my efforts like an adamantine wall.

I thus understood that there were conditions to be met to insure safety, and that *faith* alone could conquer obstacles to progress, — faith in ŏne's own soul, faith in humanity, but above all, faith in God. Presently I saw, not far off, swinging amid the swaying boughs of the silver-maples that overhung the Fay's Spring, the nest of the oriole, and three tiny heads of fledglings peeped at me over its rim. By this I comprehended that I must bring these fledglings to uphold the arch, which now fast tottered to its fall. I rebelled at such silly means in my heart;

but I was made promptly to understand, that
obedience to the divine fiat was the key of
the arch. Thereupon I promptly sought
to pass; but the sward had now become an
ocean, from whose dark depths cries of
despair and submerged warning voices addressed me. Then the Fay threw me her
distaff, for the spinner was none other than
the fairy of the spring, and she bade me have
courage.

I comprehended that I must hold the
thread of my own life in my own hands,
and bravely proceed. But as I grasped the
brittle texture it assumed the strength of
a huge cable, and leaning upon its bulk I
sought to walk the waters, when the spinner seized her distaff once more, and the
thread of my life, so treacherously grasped,
was furiously being spun out. At this moment a voice within me told me that without
prayer courage was of no avail; and almost

submerged, I cried aloud : " Lord, save me, or I perish ! "

Instantly I was raised out of the depths upon aërial wings, and I readily secured the orioles and placed their innocence as a sure support against the falling arch. At once transformed into cherubs' heads, these glorious caryatides upheld the ruin, while luminous circles played above us, like the halo that encircles a saint. As Selina stood the central figure of the group, in the far-off vista I saw the placid face of Mrs. Shirley, expressive of a religious resignation. As I wistfully contemplated the lovely scene, the distaff and the spinner floated away ; and from the woven threads of my life, like the tones of an Æolian harp, was heard the murmuring distich of prophecy : —

> " When the title of the Saint
> Crowns the house that's now attaint,
> Then the mystery is o'er,
> And great happiness in store."

I was aroused, by the incessant and mournful cry of the whip-poor-will not far distant, from the prolonged revery induced by this vision. Or had it been simply an oneirodynia, caused by the disturbed state of my mind?

CHAPTER IV.

FATA MORGANA.

BUT whether an imaginary scene had haunted my sleep, or phantasms had invaded my waking thoughts, the impression produced was painfully vivid, and I was terrified at the interpretation that would force itself upon me. For while some things were quite obscure and perplexing, there were other things that I feared might indeed be prophetic. Was not Herbert to die? What else could that dazzling apparition, almost like an apotheosis, have foretold? Then the succeeding scenes after that first grand vision clearly indicated the threatened ruin of Shirley Manor, — a ruin in which his mother and sister were involved, until I could rescue them. But the means employed to insure such measure of content as could be theirs after such irreparable loss, and the Sibylline verse, entirely mystified me ; and yet they evidently pointed out the needful conditions under which I could prop up the falling house of my friend, clear away the secret of my own life, and secure a common happiness for us all.

Amid the tumult of my brain (for I felt sure that the riddle of my destiny was entangled in this dream, if such it was) I was fully decided on one point, and that was, — not to disturb the halcyon serenity of Shirley Manor by a recital of my impressions.

Both Herbert and Selina had alluded to strange events in connection with the dreamer's first night in this room, and Herbert had confessed to having a certain belief in this superstition.

The effort that I made, assisted me to regain at least the appearance of tranquillity; and when I met my friends at breakfast, I contrived to turn the conversation into other channels with entire success.

The day brought those rural enjoyments that make a country home so delightful, and it was not until late that evening, as I was about to retire to my room, that the subject was at all alluded to. Mrs. Shirley then said : —

" Pray, Ernest, kindly occupy the room to-night which we had at first assigned to you; it is more cheerful than the one where you insisted spending last night."

" By the bye, old fellow," said Herbert, "you have never yet told us about your adventures of last night; for of course it was your duty to have a thrilling experience of some sort. I have intended asking, a score of times to-day, what befell you in that weird chamber, but we have had so many things to talk over that it has always escaped me."

" And you have saved yourself, Herbert," said I, " a disappointment; for what could you expect from such a prosaic fellow as I am ? "

" Not so prosaic, forsooth," replied Herbert with an incredulous shake of the head.

Happily for me, Mrs. Shirley at this moment interrupted him, saying : " I am greatly rejoiced that you have succeeded in curbing your imagination, Ernest, and by your good common-sense broken the spell that has so often rested over this particular spot."

" But, mamma, dear," said Selina, " such strange things have happened there, that it is quite natural we should feel just a little nervous about what takes place in that room. Only remember our precious father's dreams ! "

"Yes, I know," said Mrs. Shirley, quite agitated, "and for that very reason I am thankful when the mirror of the future is turned away from us. There are storms enough beset the dark way, as we travel on to the sunset of our days, without seeing others that we know not of in the mirage of the future."

"May I venture to ask, madam," said I, impelled by an irresistible curiosity, as I thought of my own wonderful dream, "what was the nature of Mr. Shirley's dream the first night that he spent in that chamber?"

"As the best friend of my Herbert," answered she, "I do not object to speak to you of what otherwise would be rather painful, now that the past is so blotted out for me by the loss of my beloved husband. It happened thus, Ernest. Mr. Shirley had met me in Washington; and remembering that he brought a letter of introduction to my

mother, came down in person to our dear
old homestead here, to present it. My
mother was then a widow, and I her only
child; and so we were living here alone.
It happened, however, that when Mr. Shirley
arrived, we had other guests, and it became
necessary to assign him to what was even
then called the haunted chamber, all our
other rooms being occupied. But we did
not mention to him the superstition regarding the place, as my mother was exceedingly
sensitive about it. The next morning he
startled us at breakfast by remarking to my
mother, —

"'Pardon me, madam, if I am so silly as
to revert to my dream of last night; but it
was so vivid as to seem more like a real oc-
currence than a mere hallucination. I had
just fallen asleep when there appeared to
me, seated beside the bed, an old-looking
woman who was very busily engaged in

spinning. She extended to me her distaff; and although she did not seem to speak, I understood her to say that I must hold it securely, as it contained the tangled skein of my own life, and she promised to assist me to secure a great prize. She then directed me to take the fillet and be guided by its movements. I obeyed her, impelled by a power I could not well resist; and led by this thread, that ever unravelled itself before me, I gained the lawn, which instantly became an ocean. I fancied, indeed, that I was carried over from Europe to America. Then it conducted me to that bewitching spot where your daughter took me yesterday, the Fay's Spring, where a blue-bird's nest swung high upon the topmost branch of the weeping-willow. There was one birdling in it, which I secured. Suddenly the ocean sank from view, thus closing my return to Europe, and I entered your house with my prize.'

" There was a hush at the table, for all unconsciously Mr. Shirley had adverted to our family traditions, and my mother was evidently displeased, although too courteous to censure a guest. Strange coincidences had come to pass before this, concerning that room, and mother was anxious to dis-prove the dream then and there. So turning to the negro boy Charles, who stood beside her, she said, —

" ' Charles, run quickly and bring us, if you can find such a treasure, the blue-bird's nest that swings in the topmost bough of the willow-tree that hangs over the Fay's Spring.'

" The general conversation, thus interrupt-ed, then took its course, and Mr. Shirley could not but experience a sense of mortification.

" A half hour later Charles returned, his eyes staring half out of their sockets, and handed to his mistress the blue-bird's nest, with its one fledgling within.

" ' I'se don an' foun' it, ole Miss, jis whar de gemman sawn it.'

" My dear husband," added Mrs. Shirley with a sigh, " always considered that dream to have been a true horoscope of his life. He said I was the prize, — the one fledgling which he secured, and in doing so, never re-crossed the ocean; so that on this very place was literally spun the thread of his life."

Upon hearing this strange story, so curiously similar to my own experience, it was with difficulty I could restrain my agitation, — indeed I was only able to do so by availing myself of the opportune moment to bid my friends good-night and retire to my room; and even then it was some hours before I could calm myself sufficiently to enable me to sleep. But fortunately the subject was never again alluded to during the course of my stay at Shirley Manor. In fact, I soon became so wholly absorbed by my passionate admiration for Selina Shirley, that in the various emotions that held me entranced each successive day, the wondrous vision of that first night soon ceased to be a theme of curious speculation. The Fata Morgana had already worked her spell upon me.

Only a few days remained of my visit to Shirley Manor, and I had never found courage to express my feelings in her regard. I was conscious that she must be aware of my sentiments, and Herbert too; and when I remembered how often he had left me alone with his sister, I felt sure that he had desired to assist my suit. This thought inspired me with greater confidence than any direct favor his sister had given me.

But Selina was naturally reserved; and if she had so readily given me her friendly regard, it was only as the favored chum of Herbert that she had done so. Could I venture to hope that I had aroused an interest on my own account in her affections? I tried to place the most favorable construction on every act and word of hers, but I could recall' nothing that I dared construe into positive encouragement, so guarded had been her conduct. Although I appreciated this maidenly reserve, and loved her all the more for it, yet it caused me never-ending and harassing doubt, and I dreaded to challenge certainty. Fearing to be disappointed, and thus forever destroy the dearest illusion of my life, I delayed any declaration of my love, from day to day, until the last hours of my visit drew near at hand.

The evening previous to my departure, Selina herself proposed that I should bid adieu to the Fay's Spring. Herbert said that we should at once proceed thither, remarking that he would presently join us, but not to wait for his coming. So we sauntered on until we reached the very spot where, on the first evening of my arrival, the dear girl had permitted me to call her Selina for her brother's sake. Recalling that act of condescension on her part, and remembering that the Fay's Spring was connected with the family traditions, and had also been conspicuous in my dream, with my heart beating so violently as almost to stifle utterance, I told the story of my love and poured forth the overflowing homage of my whole being. Having once dared to speak, a world of words and yearning appeals, from out the depths of a lonely heart craving for sympathy, found expression.

I was not repulsed, as I had feared to be, and I succeeded in receiving the joyful assurance that she had learned to love me, not for Herbert's sake alone, but also for myself. When, an hour later, Herbert joined us, and we hastened to inform him of our happiness, the dear boy frankly declared that no one thing — certainly nothing that concerned himself — could have delighted him more than this attachment, which presaged a common tie binding our lives. So we three, exultant in the unity of our affections, went back into the dear old homestead to beg the mother to vouchsafe her consent.

Although Mrs. Shirley must have expected such a *dénouement* to have taken place at some future time, for my devotion to her daughter had become so marked, yet she had evidently not been prepared for the impulsive suddenness of youth, and she was much distressed. As she gazed upon her beloved child as one already lost to her, she wept; and I felt like a criminal who had invaded the sanctity of a home whose broadest hospitality had been extended to him, and who had ruthlessly seized its richest treasure. But so priceless was that treasure, that I could not offer to give up my hope of possession.

"Ah, my dear madam," I said, "I beg to assure you that the consecration of a lifetime will fail to express my gratitude, if you consent to favor my suit."

Finally, Mrs. Shirley, addressing me, said :—

"After all, Ernest, you three are as yet but children, so far as a serious choice for life is concerned, and I must think over a subject of such transcendent importance for us all, before I can decide upon what is best at present. To-morrow we will confer together as regards the future."

She did not trust herself to mention the beloved name of Selina, and with tearful eyes bade me good-night; and taking her daughter's arm, retired.

"Poor mother!" said Herbert; "I fear we have been selfish, and have not thought of her. I would rather die than distress her."

"And I, dear Herbert, am the culpable one! I am an ingrate who has disturbed the serenity of the most perfect of homes! Why did you bring me within the magnetism I cannot resist?"

"Believe me, Ernest," replied he, "that I have the utmost confidence in you and affection for you; and if my mother deigns to consult me, I shall tell her that I know you will make our dear one happy. Without a doubt, my mother recognizes all your worth; but she naturally hesitates when suddenly asked to part with the dearest object left her on earth."

The last night of my visit to Shirley Manor was filled with emotions scarcely less overwhelming than those I had experienced on that memorable first night of my arrival; for the phantasms of the imagination are boundless. The next morning Mrs. Shirley, Selina, and Herbert were assembled to meet me in the library.

One thing that was especially to be admired in this little family group, was the unity of their interests. There were no bickerings, no jealousies, no concealments, but a perfect agreement of purpose. Thus Mrs. Shirley consulted with her children on all occasions, only reserving to herself the final decision after all arguments were duly weighed. This proposition of mine had met with the same open candor, and I knew that whatever the result of the conference, there would be no disguises.

"We have talked this matter over, dear Ernest," said Mrs. Shirley, "and I believe my decision expresses the common consent of my little family. I am willing that your engagement with Selina should take place, under certain conditions."

These last words recalled the "conditions" that had been imposed upon me in that all-too vivid dream, and a vague sense of impending misfortune overwhelmed me, notwithstanding the immense relief these gracious words afforded.

In a moment she resumed: "It is decided, Ernest, that more time alone is wanting to make sure that we are, none of us, mistaken; and there are many reasons why we should pause, and not be rash. Your acquaintance with Selina is almost of yesterday, and youth is proverbially volatile."

"But my love is immutable, dearest madam," I eagerly interrupted.

"Doubtless you think so now," replied Mrs. Shirley, smiling, "nor do I mistrust you; but perhaps Selina may change."

"Oh, dear mamma!" expostulated my darling.

"I do not doubt your present feelings,

nor do I doubt their stability, my children," again replied Mrs. Shirley, very gravely; "but I must insist on taking a prudent measure of time. Let Ernest return to us a year hence, after he shall have graduated; and meantime I prefer that there be no correspondence. It will be two years before he is of legal age."

"Mamma is always just right," said Herbert, approvingly.

"The condition imposed of a year's silence is a hard one," answered I, "but I gratefully accept your decision. A year hence, then, madam, I shall expect to bring to you my diploma as a graduate; and, unless your gifted Herbert intervenes, with the diploma the highest honors of the college, to be placed at your feet as some slight token of the effort I intend to make to prove worthy of the priceless boon you do not refuse me."

"I half think, Ernest," said Herbert, "that

I cráve these honors for you more than for myself; you will work with such a noble aim."

Mrs. Shirley's eyes glistened.

"Generous boys," she said, "may your purposes ever remain magnanimous! It is with a mother's love for you both that I give you my blessing."

I seized her hands and reverently kissed them. Herbert accompanied me when I returned to my own home, his mother having consented to spare him for a week, when he was to go back and give her the remainder of his vacation before re-entering college.

He was enchanted with my quaint old home, and never wearied admiring the oddities of its construction; and he took a fancy to good-hearted old Annette, who repaid his kind notice with enthusiasm, for everybody loved Herbert. His nature was essentially magnetic, and attracted all things that came within the scope of his influence. Animals were fond of him ; plants flourished if he cared for them ; an'd nothing drooped upon which the sun of his bright presence shone. Claude joined us the day after Herbert's arrival, and my guardian, Mr. King, managed to spare a day, overcrowded as he always was with work, to spend with us.

When Mr. King laid aside his " harness," as he called the red-tape routine of his life, he could be the most agreeable of men. His opinions on most subjects were so just, wise, and discriminating, as to make him a very desirable companion, especially for a young man. When a youth has capacity, he is quite sure to be aspiring, and is inclined to cherish impossible dreams as to his future achievements ; so that an older man who has good judgment and ripe knowledge of the world, can be a more useful friend than one of extraordinary talent, for in early manhood one needs sound direction rather than the infusion of a spirit of emulation. But I had an immense incentive to put forth my best efforts, by the eager desire I felt of making myself as worthy as possible of the adorable being upon whom I had centred my affections.

So introspective was my mood, that when my friends finally left me alone in the old homestead I did not experience a sense of loneliness, but rather one of relief that I might at last freely commune with my thoughts. So delightful and absorbing were these reflections, that I was like one ushered into a paradisiacal world. My deep affection for one so superior transmuted my nature and caused me to reject all alloy and seek for the highest possible excellence. I began at once to study with great diligence and to prepare myself for my classes in

advance. I was now to be a senior; and I
determined, like a true knight-errant, to lay
at Selina's feet whatever prizes were to be
won. My whole world waŝ concentred in her,
the horizon of my hopes bounded by the desire to please her, and my highest ambition to
overcome all obstacles for her. I yearned to
place the laurel-wreath of college achieve-
ment on my brow because I was hers. Had
I lived in times of old, the same devotedness
would doubtless have sought for expression
in feats of knightly prowess, when, wearing
the favor of my fair lady on my arm, I
should have brandished my trusty sword in
many a well-fought combat. My state of
feeling certainly proved that although times
had changed, the heart of a youth of nineteen desperately in love was as Quixotic as
in feudal days.

My guardian, who had noted my ardent
zeal for study, was for once misled, astute

as he was. He attributed to ambition, to
a yearning for new honors, even to a thirst
for knowledge, that assiduity and emulation
whose deepest motive existed in the affections. When he found me so immersed in
my books he supposed that I had escaped the
attractions of Shirley Manor fancy-free. I
had now, indeed, a grand secret and a grand
motive of impulsion prompting me.

One thing delighted me. Mr. King, the
most matter-of-fact of men, became enthu-
siastic when he spoke of Herbert. I could
scarcely refrain from smiling to hear him
say " that he was his mother's son, that her
rare qualities were reproduced in him, and
that men who possessed the traits of the
mother were the men who ruled the world."

I assured Mr. King " that nothing could
equal the tenderness of the relation between
this lovely mother and her gifted son, that
they were, indeed, the counterpart of each

other, and that she was in his eyes the source of all delight."

Now that my own heart was all aflame with the sacred fire, I noted with curious interest how in the case of Mr. King an early love — probably the only illusion my guardian had ever cherished — had exercised its influence upon his life, and I felt sure that its effect had been ameliorating. Had this man never loved or suffered, how could he have been so susceptible to all humane feelings, so considerate, so sympathizing, when the various sorrows of others were confided to him?

The world rarely pauses, anyhow, to do justice to the large-heartedness of the kind and good lawyer. His words, often couched in legal technicality, cause dismay; and it is not understood that these very forms are the merciful helps that are needed to clear away perplexity and save from harm. As

I looked upon my guardian at work in his daily treadmill, these thoughts were suggested as I noted the exceeding patience with which he bore countless interruptions, turning aside from the most careful analysis of nice points of law to receive the visits of the afflicted, hear their endless and often inconsequent explanations, and send them away comforted, with the assurance that their rights would be guarded, that their interests were safe in his painstaking hands. It was his high-minded conduct that first gave me to understand how noble the legal profession could be made.

. . . .

A few more weeks, and I found myself a senior, and once more fairly inducted into college life. Now my hardest work began; and I was from day to day so hard pressed for time, that I could no longer pause to analyze my emotions. But all the while, I was eagerly pressing forward to the triumphs of commencement day and the fruition of joy beyond that limit.

And Herbert, as if catching the reflection of my earnest endeavor, worked with more steady purpose than he had done before; with the result, that Claude was forced down third, and we two stood almost shoulder to shoulder, foremost in our noble strife. Now that I think over that past, I feel sure that Herbert, perhaps unconsciously, exerted himself to the degree necessary to stimulate me to the greatest possible effort, and then relaxed just one point within the climax of success. He was unselfish enough to have sacrificed himself in order to insure my highest promotion, and yet he must have wished to gratify his mother by rising to the very top round 'of the ladder. Never was son more fully the other self of a mother than he. She was ever the chiefest object of his

8

dearest affection, and he was ever the sum of all her hopes.

As the year sped on, I knew that Herbert received letters from home, by the glow of his eyes and the buoyancy of his manner, and I longed to ask him thousands of questions. But we had promised his mother to refrain from all correspondence during this one year, and in perfect faith to her and our agreement, we kept silence. I was often conscious that Herbert regarded me with wistful tenderness, as if he fully measured the extent of the trial and wished to lift the burden, if only just a little; but he was rigidly exact in the observance of his pledge, and never even alluded to Selina. Her beloved name, so dear to us both, became a blank between us.

However, only the day before the commencement, Herbert bounded into my room with the exclamation, —

"Eureka! they have come!"

"They have come —" repeated I mechanically, as if the great purport of these words exceeded my power to understand.

"Yes, old fellow," said he, laughing, and slapping me on the shoulder; "don't you care to see them — mother and Selina?"

"Care!" I almost shouted. "Merciful heavens, Herbert, where are they?"

"They have arrived, Ernest, to see us graduate and get our diplomas and receive our honors, I trust. You are to be first man, and I best man. Aha! Ernest, that's the programme."

"You torture me, Herbert! *Where* are they? — the ladies, I mean."

"Why where should they be, but in the parlor below, and you keep them waiting! You are sent for, man!"

All this was said with a merry malice of deliberation.

"Sent for!" I repeated in a dazed way, as if it were all too much happiness for the once telling.

"Sent for," said Herbert, laughing, "to be hanged, I suppose."

But almost at the instant I had recovered my wits, and the next moment found me in her presence.

How beautiful she was, how *svelte* and stately, how gracious and graceful! "And *she* would see me get my honors," kept ringing through my head, as if trumpet-toned.

Mrs. Shirley and Selina were to have seats very near the platform. What were the fifteen hundred, the huge hall full of people, to me? What recked I of the President of the United States, who was to confer our honors, of the College President, the Faculty, the dignitaries who would be present when I should be called to come forward to receive the reward of my unremitting labors? What were all these to me as compared to the appreciation of a pair of large, soft blue eyes, that would look upon me with approval? I sought my guerdon from those radiant eyes.

And the approbation of Mrs. Shirley was much to me. I could have wished for her sake to have had Herbert *primus*, for I well knew that he was more than all the world to her.

Herbert was our valedictorian, for he was above all others our silver-tongued orator. I shall never forget the pleasing effect of his address that day, — the ineffable grace of his gestures, his mellifluous voice, his affecting allusions to our approaching separation, the easy elegance of his thanks to our professors, and the eloquent peroration in which he summed up our past and our aspirations for the future. His concluding words were greeted with a perfect storm of applause. Amid the ovation that succeeded his oration, who could have foreseen even the faintest speck of calamity? and yet in the very moment of triumph my recreant imagination *would* revert to the dream in the haunted chamber, and in listening to the winning sadness of his farewell I could scarce refrain from tears. I glanced at his idolized mother, who was deadly pale, while Selina's cheeks and eyes were aglow. "What priceless, silent homage!" thought I.

Mr. King, too, was present, having, as my guardian, come to see me graduate, and they placed him beside Mrs. Shirley. As I observed them both, so calm and dignified and grave, Mr. King's fine eyes perhaps a shade darker than usual, it seemed wonderful to me that the progress of years could do its work so perfectly as to efface sentiment. I tried to place myself for a moment in the

situation of Mr. King, and to ask myself, as
a rejected suitor of Selina, if twenty-five
years later I should thus be able to sit beside her unmoved? But the impetuosity of
my youthful ardor rebelled at the very idea.
" No, no," thought I; " let endless cycles roll
their course, and I could not brook it. No,
never ! "

CHAPTER V.

THE MYSTERY UNVEILED.

AT the close of the commencement exercises, Mr. King congratulated me warmly at having taken the first honors of the class, and finished by saying, —

" I am, as you know, Ernest, always a very busy man ; but I will wait some hours and accompany you home for a day, so that we can talk over your immediate future a little. You are now a graduate and twenty years of age, and have reached a grand turning point in your career."

It was not without considerable confusion that I thanked my kind mentor, begging him to postpone his visit for a few weeks, and excuse me for the present; and I added, fairly stammering, —

"The fact is, sir, I am invited to return to Shirley Manor with our friends."

Mr. King elevated his eyebrows with a quick, nervous movement for an instant, and I knew that the exact situation had at once presented itself to him. But he only said : —

"I warned you last year, Ernest, that the attractions of Shirley Manor were more dangerous than any that Saratoga could present, and I perceive you have justified my prophecy. Success to your wooing !"

"A thousand thanks, kind sir !" said I, affectionately grasping his proffered hand.

"How much I admire his generous nature," thought I, "that can wish for others a measure of happiness he has failed to grasp for himself! He is a moral hero."

That evening we were a happy party of
four, seated on the deck of the steamer that
plied her way to Mousetown Landing. As
we moved rapidly onward, the soft white
moonlight cast its sheen upon the sparkling waves that the prow of our vessel dis-
placed, only quickly to close around us,
making a true picture of the voyage of
life. And this second time, I spent a blissful month at Shirley Manor as the accepted
lover of Selina. This ineffable boon was
gained.

Yet that ugly tyrant, Time, must still
mar my perfect joy with his effacing finger,
and point to the necessity of a still longer
probation. Mrs. Shirley insisted that our engagement must last another year. At first,
indeed, she suggested a much longer period
of trial; but Herbert came to the rescue, and
pleaded in my favor so successfully that his
mother relented, and consented to consider

the question of our marriage a year later, when I should attain my majority.

Mrs. Shirley was not aware of it, but she was invariably guided by Herbert.

" My brother," said Selina, " has such sweet, winning ways. He never appears to direct, for that my mother would not brook ; yet in his own quiet, decisive manner he explains to her what the course of action should be, as if it were her own opinion he was advocating."

" Your mother, Selina," I replied, " finds herself so reproduced in our dear Herbert, that I do not wonder if she blends his ideas with her own."

That evening I again broached the subject of a specified time for the wedding to Mrs. Shirley, finding her so well prepared by Herbert as to be quite favorable to my proposition.

" You know, dear madam," I urged with

soft insistence, " that I am wealthy, and can at once procure the luxuries of life for your peerless daughter. When I shall be twenty-one, then I am my own master, and it is my desire to travel extensively and see the world before I select a career. If Selina become my wife a year hence, and you, dear madam, will consent to accompany us, we can then go on with our education under your guiding eye."

" That plan is perfect," said Herbert; "and meantime I shall be hard at work preparing for my future triumphs as a great civil engineer. While you three are examining with critical eyes the treasures of the Old World, I shall be climbing Fame's ladder in the New."

" My Herbert," sighed the mother, fondly stroking the rich masses of his auburn hair, " be not over ambitious, I beseech thee."

" Mother mine," replied he, stealing an

arm as quietly around her waist and as lovingly as might a suitor, "as to ambition, it
is inborn. I would fain snatch the stars,
compel Nature to yield me her most treas-
ured secrets, find symbols and their full
meaning in the open map of the universe,
and then rise to the infinite, which alone can
satisfy."

As his fine eyes kindled, and the music
of his sympathetic voice still lingered in my
ear, it seemed to me that once more I felt
the presage of some near-coming woe, — or
rather, should I not say, of the glory of the
immortal fruition of his hopes!

"Ah, what is life," thought I, "but
the preparation for the harvest that Death
reaps!" And as philosophy suggested its
depreciation of the vanities that absorb us,
my glance fell upon the image of Selina,
her idolizing regard fixed upon Herbert as,
with dark shadows in her eyes, and roseate

lips apart, she sought to follow his aspiring thought.

" Ah! what is life ? " demanded my fast-throbbing heart with furious pulsations. " Life *with her* is heaven ! "

And dreamy days blended one into the other, like some soft interludes connecting harmonies, leading insensibly to the grand action of life so soon to follow. Yet who would willingly break in upon a monotone so delicious for any change ? And does this wish for the undisturbed serenity of happy hours arise from the enervating influence of passion ? Ah, no ! It is but the sigh of human nature for a return to that primal peace which was to have been ours before the divine plan was disturbed.

It was yet early in the evening preceding my departure, and the moon, being at the full, cast a broad, clear light over every object. Herbert and his mother, with an undivided heart, were exchanging loving thoughts, oblivious of our presence, when I proposed to Selina a ramble to the Fay's Spring. To stroll over the grassy sward illuminated by the mild radiance of moonlight, seemed as unreal as if we walked the waters. " The effect of moonlight is very magical," said I to Selina. " It delights, and yet it soothes."

" It prepares for the repose of the night," answered she coldly; " but its influence is too enfeebling for men."

I glanced at her with surprise. I had always felt that her spirit was of sterner mould than was Herbert's, and had often in my mind compared her movements, and even her modes of speech, to the classic models of Roman matrons. She was one of those interesting beings who charm you rather by silent appreciation than by much demonstration. I had watched the fervid glow of her countenance when listening to my conversations with Herbert, oft and again. The play of her expressive features had become for me a language to which I had given my own interpretation. Had I understood her? I knew that there was much in her character to study.

"Why should sentiment, properly directed, enfeeble men?" asked I.

"Because," she replied, "incessant, energetic action is demanded of them. To be manly is to have strength, force, and vigor."

"Then you would be ambitious for the man you love?" asked I.

"I would never consent," she replied, "to become the other self of a man who was not a leader of men. That you stood foremost in your classes meant much for me, dear Ernest," she said.

She had not often called me "dear," for she was chary of terms of affection for all except Herbert; and like a fly caught by a drop of honey, I clung to the one word.

"I will try, my Selina," I replied, "to make that first success an earnest of future triumph."

"Rather say, Ernest," she answered, "that you will compel success. To try, implies a possibility of failure. Oh, if only I were a man!" she exclaimed ardently, "my desire to soar would be illimitable. The one faint flaw in the otherwise perfect nature of my precious Herbert is, that his ambition, great as it is, fails to be boundless. I love the determination to be first, above all other resolves."

"God grant," said I, with an involuntary shudder, "that my career may never disappoint you! You are incomparably dear to me, Selina; and I must in turn confess that it was rather the desire to be worthy of you, than any force of inherent ambition, that made me strive to be *primus*."

"But," responded she, "whatever the mo-

9

tive, you did not fail. I accept the result. Success in this world is the guaranty to be secured."

By this time we had seated ourselves beside the Fay's Spring.

"To-morrow, my Selina," I said, holding within my own the little shapely hand that longed to carve out such grand destinies, "I leave you reluctantly for still another intervening year, that must lag its slow course before our union; and I promise you, my darling, that I shall fill it with action. Although to dream of you is bliss, I shall not be an inert dreamer."

"As you would please me, Ernest," answered she, "make your name great and honored among men. Perhaps you may think it strange," added she with some confusion, "but at first I thought I could never fancy you, on account of your name, — much less ever exchange the one I am so proud of, for it."

"My name!" I exclaimed in dismay, as there shot through my brain with electric force like a sudden flash relieving an utter darkness, that one last word of my aged sire, — "*nameless !*"

"Great God!" was my frenzied thought, "could there be some awful meaning in that horrible word? Could he in very sooth have meant what he said, — *nameless?*"

I mastered my rising emotion with difficulty, and with forced calmness, replied, —

"Ernest Desmarets is not as yet, my Selina, a name known to fame, as are some others. But I can be the founder of a great race. Nor yet is my patronymic all unknown. There have been men of my name who were not inconspicuous in France."

"To found a great race!" sighed she; "our Republic dismisses the idea as chimerical, and forbids us to build up inherited distinctions."

" But we can do better still, my Selina," said I, " we can enforce principles, that permit a wider and higher scope than any ever dreamed of for humanity. These are the triumphs our great Republic substitutes for the accident of birth; and these she invites us to desire."

When I led Selina to the Fay's Spring, I had intended to confide to her the mystery that had haunted, as it were, my life, and was as yet unsolved, and tell her that I hoped to find its explanation at the close of another year. But this conversation, giving me a deeper insight into a very proud nature, alarmed me to such an extent that I remained silent: I feared to be misunderstood; and moreover, a dreadful doubt seized me as to what might be the nature of my secret. I felt sure, however, that if it involved anything relating to my name, she was lost to me.

"O weird place!" thought I, "must I needs seek the shadows over this limpid water, and the entangling web of family superstitions connected with this spot, to bring new complications into my own future?"

We arose in silence, for she seemed to divine my mood, and we re-entered the house.

I left Shirley Manor and returned to my own home with an indefinable feeling of uneasiness, which I strove not to heed. Why should I create chimeras of the brain and thus disturb my peace? I had scarcely one more year to wait, when my felicity would be assured; for what greater happiness could I wish than to claim Selina as mine, and through her become closely allied to so amiable a family? Next, indeed, to the coveted possession of the woman I adored, was the satisfaction of securing a mother and a brother to love, and dear Herbert above all others, — that one friend! A sense of loneliness had until now been the severest trial of my life; but soon I was to become one of a charming home circle. Congenial minds and warm hearts were henceforth to be in unison with my own, and we should be united in one common interest. Oh, how suddenly had my future pathway been made bright!

While these and similar reflections added to my joyful exultation in case the smooth course of my love met with no adverse counter-currents, yet they only served to augment my disquiet when I was seized with apprehensions as to what my grandfather's secret might be.

Almost immediately on my arrival home Mr. King kindly came to see me, and we held a serious consultation as to my immediate future. I desired on that occasion to inform him of my engagement, but each time that I strove to express myself on this subject, an invincible repugnance restrained me from making so sacred a sentiment known. Finally, I concluded to wait until the expiration of my period of probation, when my kind guardian should be the first one to whom I would make known my happiness. Then I doubted very much if Mr. King would approve of my assuming such grave responsibilities at the very outset of life. I rather was certain that he would disapprove, and I dreaded to hear his opinion. So we talked over the plans for the coming year, which was to close his guardianship, without reference to a more distant future; and fortunately his opinions as to the course I should pursue, did not require a more extended view.

He said to me: " You have been a close and a successful student, Ernest; and as your ample means, which I am happy to inform you have been considerably increased in my hands, permit you to do so, I would advise that you should take a respite from all study, and turn for a season from books to the observation of men and manners. I think you would never regret spending the remaining nine or ten months between the present time and your majority in prolonged travel throughout the length and breadth of your own country. I am aware that this advice does not conform to the general usage, which sends our youth to make the tour of Europe in order to complete a course of study. But while I highly approve of foreign travel, and acknowledge the importance of enlarging one's views by a comparison of our own customs and laws with those of other nations, yet I do hold it to be more essential for our youth to make themselves first familiar with the institutions and the genius of our own nation."

This counsel commended itself to me as excellent, and a plan of journey was at once arranged which should fill up the intervening period until I should become of legal age. That time elapsed, I was to return and receive from Mr. King my large estate, and what in my heart of hearts I so eagerly longed to acquire, — the sealed package left me by my grandfather.

Accordingly, in the early days of October I made the tour of the New England States, spending November in Boston, and later on reaching New York, Philadelphia, Baltimore, and in December Washington. From thence I could not resist making a flying visit to Shirley Manor, where a merry Christmas, with the yule-log blazing brightly, was rapturously enjoyed.

These two or three winter evenings which I then snatched, furtively as it were, were inexpressibly delightful. They will ever

remain fondly associated with the closing
hours of my loving companionship with
Herbert. A thousandfold more attractive,
if possible, were these enchanting hours than
any the Summer, decked in all her charms,
had given us. The perfect picture of home
comfort, the fireside glow reflecting the
cheery light of our responsive hearts, the innumerable images thrown out by the fierce,
burning coals, the flickering, dancing shadows on the walls, the sense of exclusiveness
when the lustrous sheen of heavy drapery
shuts us in from the contrasting discomfort
without, while the furious blast shrieks in
vain. We only draw the closer around the
centre table, where a magnetic influence we
would not dispel falls upon us from the
mildly beaming lamp and the pale glimmer
of the waxen candles. Amid the cheerfulness of such a scene my Selina shone forth
like some resplendent gem placed alone

within its setting, refracting millions of rays, and dazzling our eyes with the brilliancy that environed her. Never, never, had I seen her so entrancing!

At the time of my arrival I was especially welcomed, as I found the little family group in anxious consultation over a proposition recently made by Mr. King to Herbert. It had been the first intention of Herbert to go to St. Louis and there accept an offer from a famous civil engineer to become his secretary, with a view to the ultimate adoption of that profession. But Mr. King had been greatly impressed by the remarkable talent that Herbert had evinced when he delivered the valedictory address, and foresaw that he would attain great distinction at the Bar, and later on in public life as an orator. And perhaps, without being conscious of it, my guardian had wished to attract, that he might share his own life, the gifted son of the only

woman whom he had ever loved.   But whatever were the motives, hidden or manifest,
he had offered Herbert such very handsome
terms to induce him to enter his office that I
at once urged their acceptance, especially as
a junior partnership was promised so soon
as Herbert should be admitted to practice.
Herbert reluctantly decided to accept, for
the career of a civil engineer had pleased
his imagination, as being full of action
and affording much scope for talent and
enterprise.

We left Shirley Manor together on New
Year's Eve for Washington, where the Sena-
tor from Maryland, who was an old friend of
Mrs. Shirley, had invited us to accompany
him in making various New Year's calls.
It was our first glimpse of social official
life at the national capital, and we found
the picture presented both curious and
interesting.

But that day will ever remain deeply marked in my heart of hearts, as being the one in which I parted from my loving friend, my brother in affection. Herbert left with high hopes of a prosperous future, one that was to lead to eminence in the career he had adopted, and I started anew on my travels. Our hand-shakings were as fervent as our feelings; and with many a blithe word and no cloud of premonition, we parted.

" Pray write me often, old fellow," said Herbert, — " that is, if three letters a day to Selina spare you an odd moment for a friend."

" Herbert, you are a great tease," I responded. " May your punishment be to fall headlong in love, and right speedily, my boy ! "

" Not while mother lives," he quickly answered; " we two are one. No need of solace other than her love."

"God bless you! God bless you!" we both exclaimed, not willing to show all the emotion we felt.

I, never recking the sorrow that was in store, pursued my journey, spending the winter in the Southern States, sailing from Charleston to Cuba, and from the Havana to New Orleans, and thence going to St. Louis. The ensuing month of May found me at Chicago. Then I took a tour of the lakes; and finally Niagara and Canada filled up the measure of ten months' travel marked out for me.

And now the culminating period of all my cherished hopes drew near at hand; the five years which had seemed so interminable to look forward to had melted into the irrevocable past, and I had gained the goal. Having reached the grand climacteric of my hopes and fears, — my three times seven, — my twenty-first birthday, the critical hour which I had so long wished for, found me with the sealed package at last given into my own hands.

With a nervous dread of interruption, I retired to my room and locked myself in before I ventured to open the parcel. The trembling hand in which the superscription had been written had a pathetic meaning, indicating as it did the feebleness of those last days of my grandfather's life. I was painfully reminded of that sultry summer's afternoon, when the cyclone of my passionate demonstration had prostrated the faint glimmer of life that at eighty-one was flickering in the socket.

" Eighty-one and twenty-one ! " thought I. " Are these periods to be coincidental agreements in our lives, with two generations intervening, over which this mystery has cast its upas-shade ? " With dazed senses, I broke the seals and perused the following :

MY BELOVED ERNEST, — The day when you will read this, and for the last time hear, as it were, my voice speaking to you from out the tomb, you will also enter into the full possession of my worldly goods, with which I shall endow you with a loving heart and my paternal blessing.

Would to God that I could exempt you, my dear grandson, from bearing also a sorrowful inheritance, which has through life depressed me, — one which may perchance seem but an unsubstantial chimera to you, but which has embittered my existence! How can I tell you, my Ernest, that the name we bear is only that of a maternal ancestress, and that the cognomen of our family is cruelly hidden from us? Yet, my child, from what I do know of my father's career I have every reason to believe that we are well descended and of honorable lineage; but I have no means of establishing this fact with certainty.

All that I know of our origin is this: My father was a military man, and served in the army during the reign of Louis XV. with distinction. After the treaty of peace was signed at Paris in February, 1763, he returned home, but in a short time departed, in consequence of an angry dispute with his father, declaring that he should never hear from him again. At the same period my father dropped his surname, only retaining that of his mother, and came to Paris.

Already, with the advent of Louis XVI., unhappy France had become so agitated that it was an easy thing to hide one's identity in that city. Having satisfied the aged Comte de Maurepas, who was a friend of his mother's family, as to who he was, he recommenced his army life and was given a place of trust at Court, where some years later the Revolution that burst forth in all its fury found him loyal and true.

Soon after his arrival in Paris, my father married, under his name of Desmarets, Rosalie, the lovely daughter of Dr. Cruchet, a distinguished surgeon. There was at first some objection made by Dr. Cruchet on account of his being a stranger; but upon receiving a confidential communication from M. de Maurepas, consent was given. I was the only child of that marriage, and had the prospect of a good career, as my father was an officer well received in good society, and my maternal grandfather was very wealthy.

One day, when I was a lad of eighteen, my

10

father said to me: "Ernest, I intend at some time, after I am no more, that you shall resume your true name; but you are as yet too young to have my full confidence."

He then narrated to me exactly what I now tell you, but no more, — except that he spoke with great tenderness of his mother, whose maiden name he said was Estelle Desmarets.

I was a proud boy. Like most only children, I had been greatly petted, and doubtless spoiled. I was all impatience to know who I was. But my father was a man of haughty bearing and fierce temper, and I did not dare to press him with a single question. However, I looked forward to my becoming a man of twenty-one, as the happy period when my history was to be made clear.

Alas! my dear son, an adverse fate decreed otherwise; for two years later, when I was twenty, such a fierce outburst of Revolutionary frenzy devastated France that I fled the country in dismay. I succeeded in reaching a seaport in safety, and secreted myself in a vessel about to sail for America. Of my career in the land of my adoption you are well informed, and you also know that it has not been without useful and honorable results.

Upon my arrival in the United States I at once wrote to my mother, informing her of where I was; but in those days it was an affair of months to cross the Atlantic in a sailing vessel, and events in France moved with terrible speed. My poor father, despite his gray hairs and faithful service, had been one of the very first victims of the guillotine after the execution of his sovereign, Louis XVI., and my mother had died broken-hearted. Dr. Cruchet had likewise succumbed to the weight of years and such deep sorrow, but had left me his heir in case I could ever be found. In effect, after the Revolution had expended itself, I was informed that the estate was mine.

But meanwhile I had married in this country, and formed ties that had endeared me to the generous nation that had so kindly received a fugitive; and listening to the entreaties of your grandmother, I determined to make her people my people, and remain where I was.

But the knowledge that I was in ignorance of my true surname weighed upon me so heavily that I at one time returned to Paris in order to try and find out who I was. The only clew I held was through what my father had told me of his confidences to the aged Comte de Maurepas. I knew also that he bore one of his mother's names.

The old minister of the unfortunate king was then no more, and the surviving members of his family, whom I succeeded in finding, could give me no information whatever. In fact when I made known my mission I was stared at as one demented, and I had only the mortification of hearing the question in an incredulous tone: "What, sir, in search of your *name?*" So that the few to whom I confided my misery only made me the more wretched. I know nothing about my family, either what part of France they came from, or who they were. The frightful convulsions of the Revolutionary storm seemed to have destroyed every landmark which might have assisted me in hunting out the records of my mother's family. Had they, too, been swept away?

I never can tell you, Ernest, how this consciousness of irreparable loss has weighed upon me through life. I have in vain reasoned with myself upon the painful subject. I sink into the tomb still questioning the unknown. Be not dismayed at the legacy of doubt I leave you. I pray God that you may at least succeed in shaking off the phantasm that has harried me, and, despite much to be thankful for, made my life wretched. I trust even that, being an American bred and born, you will have the courage of a full manhood to rise above and beyond all inherited distinction, and carve for yourself either the name you bear, or any other you may care to assume, on a high pinnacle of fame.

But, oh! my Ernest, I cannot, even from out the sepulchre of all my hopes, express to you the intense longing that consumes me in your behalf, that you may, by some merciful Providence, be permitted to lift the veil that hides you from yourself. May you find your lost name, and not fall, as I must do, into a grave which can only be inscribed as *nameless*.

The fatal paper dropped from my nerveless hands, and the bitter words " lost name," and that concluding " nameless," crushed me like a sentence of irrevocable doom. I felt that the guillotine of fate had fallen upon me, and blighted my dearest hopes in life ; for ah! too well I knew that the proud Selina would never share the destiny of a miserable being who was so abject as to be nameless.

Then came the temptation to say nothing about this wretched complication. Without having had the intention to withhold my confidence, but from a natural sensitiveness, I had refrained from unveiling to any one this mystery that had surrounded me. Why not bury my heavy burden in the tomb of the dead past, as even my poor grandfather had suggested I might do, and arise, like the phœnix, unshackled, bearing a new name and free? Why not? Already the peace of one life had been blasted ; was not this expiation sufficient for the sin of an ancestor who had failed in filial obedience? What Nemesis required the extermination of a race?

Oh, how I longed to yield assent to the blandishments of this sophistry! Methought I stood between two diverse paths, each claiming my choice. On the one side was the narrow, thorny, dark way, sharp set with difficulties, but which my inner consciousness told me was the road of unflinching rectitude and undeviating adherence to virtue. While on the other a broad, flowery mead presented itself, embellished with every charm to please the senses, but where were hidden pitfalls that might ensnare one to ruin.

In the transport of my heated imagination, once more seemed to appear before me the spinner of Shirley Manor, now transformed into one of the veritable Parcæ, with uplifted shears ready to cut short the thin-spun thread of my existence.

The inner combat was long and bitter; but at last my good angel triumphed, and I determined to act with entire candor and leave the result, even if it involved the wreck of all my cherished hopes, with a higher Power. I had not been trained in habits of prayer; but there are supreme moments in every life when the soul bows before the great Unseen, seeking strength to do the right, and imploring merciful consideration for human weakness.

"O thou great Unknown!" I exclaimed, "O God my creator, assist me to find the truth and be steadfast to uphold it!"

Heartfelt prayer, in whatever language it may be couched, always brings peace; and I gained the strength I needed for self-conquest. Thus I was enabled to resist the specious temptation to hide my secret from the woman whom I sought to make my wife, and I had the moral courage to make known to her just as they were all the facts regarding the mystery of my family history.

In conclusion, I left it to her to decide, in these words: —

"My darling, — if mine I may longer be permitted to claim you, — my story is told, and my happiness rests in your gracious hands. Will you, can you, knowing all I know, consent to share with me the name by which I am called, one that has never been questioned or dishonored, yet to which in reality I am not entitled. Will you trust to my unremitting endeavors to make you happy and honored, and to cause this name to be respected among men and worthy to be transmitted to posterity? Be compassionate, Selina, and do not, I implore you, reject the substance of happiness for illusory dreams.

But if you can not, or will not, make this sacrifice for my sake, I free you from your promise of marriage, which all unwittingly I accepted from your dear lips, in answer to the fondest protestations of fealty, which I again renew if you will still accept them. God above knows how I have loved you, and shall ever love you. Be merciful, then, Selina, and do not sacrifice on the altar of ambition your devoted   ERNEST.

The fateful missive was sped, and I had but to await the confirmation of my doom, — for doomed I knew myself to be; I understood all too well that a spirit of uncontrollable ambition dominated the mind of Selina Shirley. There could not have been much time lost in the decision, for not many days had elapsed before the answer was received.

I can only compare the instant preceding the one in which I opened this letter, to that moment of duration in which some poor wretch feels the noose adjusted which in another turn is to swing him out into an eternity of despair. Her words were not many; had they cost her a heart-break?

She wrote me : —

ERNEST, — I honor the transparent candor of your soul, and I feel that if this dreadful mystery could find its solution, your name would be vindicated. Would to God that this bitter, bitter chalice could have been presented in any other shape! But I cannot consent to yield the proud old English name I bear, for a nonentity. Ernest, believe me, had the trial been an endurable one, I would have sought for your sake to support it. Had it involved, for instance, loss of fortune, I would have cheerfully shared the cross with you and helped you seek for recognition. But, oh! Ernest, what hope can exist in endeavor, what fruition can we look forward to, if — pardon me, Ernest, I only mention it in self-justification — if one is *nameless?* I am unhappily so constituted that the abhorred thought would kill me. I beg you, Ernest, do not distress Herbert by any knowledge of this deep sorrow that has fallen upon us. No other love shall ever fill the place I had promised should be yours, Ernest; but in future my hopes, my life, must be centred in Herbert. Do not deem me cruel; I am as I am, and I cannot be otherwise. Ambition is the one devouring flame that consumes the heart of

SELINA SHIRLEY.

CHAPTER VI.

PROVIDENCE AT THE HELM.

THE severe tension of this interval of uncertainty had been so painful, that although the result blasted my hopes of a serene and blissful future, yet, compared to the anguish of uncertainty I had endured, it was a relief to know the worst. So strangely constituted is the human heart, that suspense is perhaps the extremest torture to which it can be subjected.

I now beheld my most cherished anticipations of happiness disappear at one blow. I paused to measure the extent of the calamity. During three of the best years of my life I had looked forward to the love of this

woman as my richest guerdon. For her sake
I had fed the fires of ambition with incessant
and toilsome effort, until I had won the first
prizes of the collegiate course. But it was
evident that my love, my devotion, had not
been the one object of her life. I had not
held the first place in her affections, for
Herbert had never ceased to be nearest and
dearest to her. Why should I, amid the
wreck of my desires, longer disguise from
myself what I had really known ever since
that conversation at the Fay's Spring, — the
fact that ambition was in very sooth, as she
had so forcibly expressed it, "the one devouring flame that consumes the heart of Selina
Shirley"? She had never attempted to deceive me in any way; for did she not tell
me that she had thought to find a leader
of men in me? My strange secret had been
aimed at the very Shechinah of her soul.
She had built up the most extravagant

expectations of an impossible future, and she fancied that their fulfilment in me had become futile.

Yet she loved me. She strove, it is true, to hide this love from herself, and to cling the closer to her aspirations, through Herbert. It was, indeed, a desolating grief to lose her, and almost an equal pain to look forward to that blurred friendship which, all explanation debarred, must inevitably arise between my friend and myself.

And must I lose Herbert too? Far better that I had never met Selina. Yet I was not crushed. I was conscious of upright conduct, of having done no wrong, and of that self-approbation that accompanies a duty bravely met. There were, after all, no dark shadows to abash me, no giants athwart my path to turn me back.

As an American youth I could not share the depression that my poor grandfather had experienced in consequence of an ignorance of his surname. He was, in fact, a Frenchman born and bred, and in early life up to manhood had breathed an atmosphere that caused him to give a deep significance to the loss of his name.

Selina Shirley also was rather an English than an American girl. Her father had been a younger son of a noble family, and in temperament a dreamer. He had strongly impressed his daughter with his ideas in the isolated life they had led. Then her mother was a Southern woman, and they both were natural aristocrats, and had, moreover, been influenced by the oligarchic sentiments which slavery creates.

But I was essentially a Northerner, born and reared in one of the great free States of the Union, with no influences, no traditions of the effete Old World to hamper me, no barnacles attached to weigh me down. I was a free man, my own master absolutely, wealthy too, — for wealth was not to be despised. I could be influential, and I would be, despite all obstacles. My pride was roused and, like some wild beast springing forth from its hidden lair, ready to do battle.

"A nonentity forsooth!" I exclaimed; "I will prove to this proud girl, enchantress as she is, that I have, even despite her, a career, an individuality of my own."

After all, it is the essence of one's being, and not any nominal distinction, that makes the man. Let us turn over the pages of history and see whose are the names that glow high above all others, like the fixed stars of heaven, the men who have been the autocrats of nations and have regulated the affairs of the world. Who originated *their* names? Who cares? Who asks?

Titles and emblazoned figures file in endless procession; but the men, the master

minds who direct the glittering pageant of
the world's renown, are the truly illustrious.
It is not even the despot who rules, but the
power that directs his brutal resolve. Great
names, it is true, shine forth like the sun,
transmitting light adown the ages and stimu-
lating to noble action. But the men who
inherit them with such insolent pride do
not likewise inherit a transmitted glory of
great deeds, but rather resemble the jackdaw
strutting in borrowed plumage.

How seldom do great deeds uphold great
names! Heroes, like poets, are heaven-born,
and come not of earth's lineage. " Let me
rather," thought I, " like a true American, re-
joice that I have to make a name for myself.
The world eagerly accepts any name that
benefits humanity."

But far beyond all selfish ambition is the
sublime spectacle religion presents. He who
has faith in the unseen prefers to annihilate

11

himself here, in order to be great hereafter. There are thousands upon thousands of men and women in religious Orders who voluntarily bury their names out of sight in this world, and assume those of the models they strive to imitate. What a wonderful irony of divine selection, that exalts the humble and casts down the proud! For we find the names that are revered as saintly, belonged to those who embraced nothingness and humiliations.

Thus did I struggle with conflicting thoughts, that, like fierce counter-currents, tossed me to and fro. I bent to the storm that threatened to overwhelm me; but finally I arose out of the awful trial strengthened and superior to my former self. I had gained a higher plane, for I now sought to cast aside forms and grasp the essence of things; and I resolved that if I must bear the pain of living without love or tenderness or sympathy, I would, by honorable action and constancy of purpose, compel respect. No man, no woman, could deprive me of this inalienable right.

Several weeks passed by, during which I remained at my old home, striving to acquire fuller mastery over myself; out of which persevering effort came, little by little, a firmer mind and a calmer soul. I was aware that I could not for any length of time remain in this deep seclusion without causing much curious comment, and I desired to lose no time in deciding what course I was to pursue. It was, indeed, a difficult problem that presented itself, involving an absolute change in all my previous projects.

But I could not as yet decide upon anything definite. All my plans had been so frustrated, so entire was the ruin of the fair structure I had built, that, like Archimedes,

I sought in vain for the fulcrum needed to recommence.   My soul, ever groping, cried out: " Let me but find a place to stand on, and I will lift my cross ! "

But, as it constantly occurs in this world, while we are in vain planning, suddenly Divine Providence takes the helm and makes the move in the right direction to extricate us.   Thus, as I was searching about in the obscurity that closed around me, feeling as yet too prostrate to rush into the combat of external affairs that awaited me, yet not knowing how to fill up the interval of time I needed, the way was made straight.

My college chum Claude, for whom I had always had much friendly regard, came to see me.   His home was in New Orleans, where he had in the past year studied law in the office of a prominent advocate; and some French claims against houses in this country had been intrusted to him.   In the course of

his investigations he found that he must go
to France and seek a personal interview
with his clients, in order clearly to adjust
various disputed points. He had taken passage in a steamer that was to sail in a few
days for Havre, and ran up to spend twenty-
four hours with me.

My mind was at once made up. Mr.
King had given over my affairs in perfect
business shape into my hands. There was
nothing to delay my movements, no one to
consult. I decided to accompany my friend.
Claude was delighted at a step taken so suddenly, that while one day I sat alone in my
room holding ceaseless debate with myself
and asking never-ending questions of the
future, the very next day found me, as night
closed in, afloat in the swirl of the restless
ocean.

Yet its troubled motion was restful compared to the turbulence that had shaken my

breast. This precipitate departure suited me well. I could not refrain from sending one hurried word of loving farewell to Herbert, in which I mentioned that my departure was not in conflict with his sister's expressed wishes, — from which I supposed he would conjecture our engagement to be broken, — and I assured him of my immeasurable and undying affection. A kind word of thanks was also sent to my worthy guardian, in which I gave him my Paris address, in case any business communication required it; and there was nothing more to be done.

In what a small compass move our hopes and fears! Most human lives turn upon a narrow axis, however broad may be the circle of their action. The world's pressure is centrifugal; but the centripetal force that comes from our affections overrules.

A long and stormy passage was a godsend to me, for I needed counteracting influence to take me out of myself; but at last we landed in safety at Havre.

As neither time nor place was of consequence to me, I told Claude that, having no plans formed, I would, for a time at least, drift onward, guided by his movements. As I recalled the history of my race so far as it had been made known to me, it was not without profound emotion that my feet pressed for the first time the soil of France. Under what different circumstances had my grandfather fled from its shores more than half a century ago! Yet even then, the same mystery that induced him to return a score of years later, in hopes to find its solution, had also in a certain way caused me to leave my native country.

"And why not," flashed into my mind, "have in view the same object that lured him hither?"

Alas! it is but too true that there is a

fainter prospect for me than there was for
him to solve this ever-elusive enigma. A
longer time has now elapsed, and all the
actors of the drama must have disappeared.
But I could not fail to be impressed by
the fact, that without premeditation I had
crossed the ocean and come to France. Ah,
let me venture to see in this step the direction of a merciful Providence! But with
this flattering thought, the fascinating image
of Selina so disturbed my imagination that
I strove to dismiss the subject as impracti-
cable and no longer to be entertained.

Of course we made Paris our first' object-
ive point, as every one must do who enters
France. Claude, like myself, was, as I have
before said, of French descent, and this was
his first visit to the land of his forefathers.
He was very naturally eager to see Paris, and
I was more interested in doing so than I
was willing to admit to myself. I established

myself at an excellent hotel, and decided to remain in Paris while Claude took various excursions in the vine-growing districts, where his clients resided.

Several months thus elapsed, during which I managed to occupy the time very fully in the examination of the numerous objects of interest that this vast and astonishing city presents. Finally, however, I began to re-lapse into that listless state of mind I so much dreaded. So one evening, Claude having returned to Paris, I proposed to him a change of scene, and begged that he would accompany me in making the tour of Europe. He said that if I would wait a few days until he could complete some matters of business which were nearly settled, he would gladly go with me. Indeed, he had recently received letters of credit, which his father had generously sent him to use for that purpose.

Finally, on the very eve of our departure, our arrangements having been made to go to Nice, Claude received a letter from a gentleman, the owner of extensive vineyards in Burgundy, who wished to confer with him regarding business arrangements with some American houses. As we had intended passing through Burgundy, and as M. Savary resided at his villa near Dijon, which town was in our route, Claude asked me kindly to accompany him.

So far from objecting to this delay, — for time had no specific value to me, — I assured my friend that I should rather enjoy a glimpse of life in the provinces. Thus we left Paris together; and traversing the charming valley of the Seine, we soon entered the famous province of Burgundy, and stopped at Dijon, that nestles at the base of its vine-clad hills.

Here, awaiting our arrival, was an agree-

able gentleman of middle age and very
suave manners, who introduced himself as
M. Savary. He insisted that we should
both become his guests; and entering his
carriage, we were rapidly driven to his coun-
try-seat, which was beautifully situated a
league distant from Dijon, on an eminence
that commanded a fine view of that important old town, and of the fertile plain in-
tersected by the rivers Ouche and Suzon,
which here have their confluence.

The villa was of modern construction, perhaps a little too new and pretentious, but
planned with exceeding care. It was a pleasing specimen of the residence of a wealthy
man of the *bourgeoisie*, or middle classes of
the country. It was very evident that money
had not been spared, — and indeed this re-
minder that it was costly was its defect.
For had the walks been less elaborate, the
pretty pavilion in front of the house not

quite so fine, the artificial lake less exact in its outlines, the hedges not trimmed in such fanciful shapes, so that one could for a moment forget the gardener and enjoy the hedge, — had Nature, in a word, been less hampered, more would have been left to the imagination to enjoy. The house presented an attractive façade, looking upon the garden; and we entered by a double flight of very high steps, the platform where they united forming a pretty balcony at the front door. It was a spacious double house, with high basement, two stories, and mansard roof. All its apartments were light and airy.

I love to recall the place, for it is so intimately connected with one of the most memorable and happy days of my existence, that every feature of the cheerful home stands out in my memory bathed in a flood of sunshine.

Dinner was announced soon after our arrival, and was admirably served. The fine wines of Burgundy formed a principal topic of conversation, and we had some of very choice vintage offered. The family consisted of our host and Madame Savary and two young people, — a son and a daughter, who had they been Americans would probably have led the conversation, but being in France, they remained perfectly quiet in the presence of their seniors.

The one figure of the household, however, to whom every one paid unlimited deference, was the aged father of M. Savary, who, I was informed with much pride, was verging on to ninety, and could still honor them by taking a place at table. Once or twice during the dinner he mumbled a few words, when instantly all other conversation ceased, every one being attentive to catch his meaning.

Dear old gentleman! I love to remember just how he looked, as seated in a huge *fauteuil,* his slippered feet carefully placed on a velvet cushion, his stout gold-headed cane held between his knees, upon which he leaned forward now and then when he was talking, and his silver corona of a few straggling white hairs surmounting a high forehead.

I have always had an affection for the aged, and I placed myself very near his chair, as he reminded me not a little of my own dear grandfather, and it was grateful to me to seat myself at his side. He noticed my attention, and seemed pleased with it, and asked his son to mention my name more clearly, as he had not fully caught the sound, for he was very deaf.

" M. Desmarets, father," said my host.

" Des-ma-rets, Des-ma-rets," he muttered several times to himself, as if striving to re-call a banished train of thought.

" My father," explained our host, " evidently recalls your name, sir. He has a very wonderful memory for the persons whom he knew when he was young, although he pays little heed to those he meets now. It is seldom he notices a stranger. Perhaps you resemble some early friend of his youth."

But now the old gentleman moved his lips as if he would begin to talk. A little bent forward, leaning slightly on his cane and with his eyes fixed on vacancy, it seemed as if he were communing with another world, and not addressing himself to those who so respectfully listened to his every word.

How weird and strange are the ways of extreme old age, always seeming to reach over the boundary line and ignore the realities of the present!

We waited a moment, but he did not speak, and I could not endure the suspense of his silence. So I said very quietly and

slowly, and in a tone of voice to make myself
understood : —

"Have you ever before heard my name,
sir? Desmarets." I repeated, "Desmarets."
He started, bent an inquiring gaze upon me,
and repeated, —

"Desmarets ! oh, yes ; Ernest Desmarets — "

I felt myself rigid with the fear that he
might pause, for now I knew that the name
was familiar to him.

He hesitated still, searching my features
as if to catch the fast-coming recollections
in their light; then went on, —

"Estelle Desmarets was a beautiful woman, — she who was the orphan ward of the
haughty old Marquis, and her *dot* was a
handsome fortune. But the young Marquis
little cared for her *dot*, which, however, recon-
ciled the father to the marriage. He did not
half like to have his son marry any one but

the highest, and of the *ancien régime.* Well,
the world looked very bright to the young
people, who in due time were left at the old
castle, at the death of the venerable Marquis,
with a son and daughter of their own. The
daughter, Estelle, was good and lovable ; but
the son, Ernest, was as his grandfather had
been, very overbearing and wilful. He soon
gave them trouble, and entered the army
against their wish. He served under Louis
XV., and came home, having won a medal.
Then his father said he must marry the
richest heiress in Burgundy, the Comtesse
de Brienne, who, however, was neither young
nor pretty. There was a furious quarrel, and
it all ended by the son swearing a big oath
that he would leave home and never be.
heard of again. That night he disappeared,
and never could be found. His poor mother,
she drooped and died broken-hearted, and
his father — "

12

During this recital of what I knew must be my family history, my agitation gradually increased, until at this point it became uncontrollable, and I cried out in a hoarse voice:

"For God's sake, sir, the name! Oh, tell me the name!"

The old man, startled by my unfortunate exclamation, instantly lost the thread of his long soliloquy, gazed at me with a vacant stare, shook his head, sighed, seemed to forget everything, and lapsed into silence. Soon after they conducted him to bed.

And once more, by my foolish eagerness, my indiscretion, I had deprived myself of the knowledge I was so anxious to gain! But now I stood upon the very threshold of the unknown, with the veil partly lifted, and holding at least a clew that might serve to guide my investigations. I felt perfectly sure that this aged man could reveal the secret of my family name if his thoughts could again be led into the same channel, from which my unguarded vehemence had diverted them.

Trusting to find the assistance I needed, I requested the kind indulgence of my host, and related to him and to Claude, as succinctly as I could, the circumstances of the painful mystery that surrounded me regarding my name. I did not connect Selina in any way with my history, only mentioning the contents of my grandfather's package, and saying how unavailing had been our search in retracing our lineage.

M. Savary was deeply interested and Claude much touched by the sad events narrated, and we were all quite sure that the aged parent of our host would be able to explain the mystery, in case he could again be led to continue the same narrative.

" It is most unfortunate," said our host, " that the train of ideas was interrupted. But my father is an encyclopædia as to knowledge of family traditions of the last century, and we will try to arouse the same reminiscences to-morrow. I beg you, my dear sirs," added he, addressing us, " to remain as my guests until father can recall the name we are anxious to hear."

We thanked him heartily for the hospitable invitation, and I was grateful to accept his aid.

It is needless to say that I passed a sleepless night, my heart agitated with a thousand conflicting emotions. Nor did I omit devoutly to implore the Divine Being to vouchsafe to make clear all obscurity. Never before had I so fully recognized the guidance of a Higher Power in the events of my tangled life, or felt so entirely my dependence on the protection of Heaven. My very coming to this place was purely providential. It seemed as if the day would never dawn. When I thought of the feeble tenure of life, the attenuated thread of those ninety years, I trembled. The slightest excitement would snap asunder the dim light that now flickered, and must so soon expire.

At an early hour I awaited his coming; but he was later than was his wont, and it was almost high noon before he could be gently led to the same chair. His son wisely thought that the safest plan was to arrange everything in precisely the same order as during the evening previous, then place me at his side, and again renew the conversation at the point where it had been broken off.

At first the nonogenarian was as wilful as a little child. He wished, he insisted, upon being rolled.about the grounds in his reclining-chair; but finally, to my inexpressible joy, our plan was effective.

A few moments after I had taken my place beside him, his son said very gently, but so that the old gentleman could understand, —

"Father, this is Ernest Desmarets."

The old man started, glanced at me; then seemed to forget my presence, and looked blank. Great beaded drops stood upon my brow, such was my anguish of suspense; but I dared make no sign.

M. Savary tried again.

"Father, Estelle Desmarets was a very beautiful woman, was she not?"

"Yes," replied the aged parent; "but Ernest broke her heart. He was her only son. May God forgive him! There must have come some punishment on his race for his disobedience to his parents. Even the old Marquis never looked so proud again. 'We must keep up the name,' he said, and he made Estelle, their lovely daughter, marry her cousin of the same name. So she became the countess. But somehow a blessing never came of it to the race, for only a daughter was born of this alliance, and she has never married. The poor old lady lives alone, and the last of a noble lineage is this Mademoiselle de Saint-Sorlin."

So saying, as if exhausted, he leaned his head forward, rested his chin on the knob of his gold-headed cane, and once more lapsed into silence.

My veins were swollen, and my tongue cleaved to the roof of my mouth during this prolonged agony of expectation; and as at last the longed-for name was uttered, I grew dizzy, and reeled, as if falling.

The first words that recalled me, as it were, to myself, so dazed was I by the whole situation, was the respectful salutation of my amiable host, who said with *empressement*, —

"Allow me to be the first to congratulate the Marquis de Saint-Sorlin."

"How wonderful are the ways of Providence," I exclaimed, "who has at last forgiven the sin of my ancestor and restored his unworthy descendant to that birthright of which his filial disobedience had deprived us! And next to God, my grateful thanks are due to you and your venerable parent, my dear sir."

CHAPTER VII.

THE RIDDLE SOLVED.

IN the animated conversation that ensued, upon this dramatic *dénouement*, M. Savary informed us that his father had in early life owned a small vineyard in the south of Burgundy, and he had heard him say that it was his habit to reserve some of his choicest wines for the use of several old families, whose castles were not far distant; that doubtless the history of this particular house had been well known to him. He must, indeed, have seen various members of the family at different times.

Although it seemed like a somewhat Quixotic adventure, M. Savary advised that we should at once seek Mademoiselle de Saint-Sorlin, and he proposed to accompany Claude and myself on the journey, saying that he had not the slightest doubt but that we should find his father's recollections of events correct in every particular.

I had the less hesitancy in making myself known to the sole living representative of my race, as I had no intention of seeking to deprive her of either land or money, but rather wished to assist her, in case she needed me in any way. Indeed, for reasons too sacred to make known to my companions, it was all-important that I should, if possible, establish my claim to my new-found name.

Our plans having been speedily made, we left the next morning, a merry party of three; for M. Savary proved a most agreeable addition to our company. My heart was light and buoyant, and the world now seemed clothed in prismatic hues of brilliancy and loveliness. Once more I allowed myself a renewal of those dreams of felicity I had determined forever to banish from my life. I thanked God that he had accepted the sacrifice of my will to him, and that in his mercy he had spared me the threatened desolation, when I had resolved to endure the worst. Truly, it is not the external world that changes, but our own interior dispositions which form the kaleidoscopic glasses that give their hue to every object.

We passed by Mâcon, and finally reached Lyons. At this city we procured horses, intending to make the rest of our journey on horseback. Crossing the Rhone, we entered a picturesque valley closely hemmed in by mountains, where, after a romantic ride of several leagues, we reached the little village of Nuits de Saint-Sorlin, just as the most gorgeous sunset-clouds irradiated the distant snow-clad summit of Mont Blanc.

We found a quaint old hostel, where the innkeeper managed to make us comfortable, especially when he learned that the object of our coming was to pay our respects to Mademoiselle de Saint-Sorlin. Like most men of his class, he was very loquacious, and gave us of his own accord many particulars about this lady which we were glad to hear. He said that she was much beloved, and accessible to all who needed her aid.

" In fact," he added, " Mademoiselle is the good angel of our village, and no one in trouble ever came to her in vain. But now she is growing quite old, and of late years we do not often see her amongst us. She is rheumatic too, and walks with difficulty. We often wonder who will be her heir, because when she dies the race dies out with her, — unless, indeed, the descendants of the Marquis who went away saying that he never would return, should come back some fine day and claim their rights. Suzette and I often talk it over winter nights.

"But Mademoiselle always says that he will yet appear, — which makes some people call her eccentric. She comes once a year, on the feast-day of the saint, to our church of St. Anthony, and has a Mass said for the repose of the soul of the young Marquis, who was not heard from after he left Saint-Sorlin in such great wrath; and also, she says, to ask St. Anthony to send back the lost heir. And she declares that he will return before she dies, because she has every year for fifty years prayed for this favor, and she knows that finally her prayers will be answered.

"But as each year rolls round, and no one has ever heard the faintest whisper of news, it has fallen into a proverb. When one means that a thing can never happen, we

say: 'Yes, when St. Anthony sends back
the lost heir!' But yet Mademoiselle does
not cease to have faith. She only says:
'Patience, my friends!'

"And you are here, sirs, in good season,
for to-morrow is the anniversary she cele-
brates; and you cannot fail, at nine o'clock,
to see her arrive, carried in her sedan-chair
(the very one her grandmother used) to the
church-door. My grandfather can remember
when as a mere lad he would notice the old
Marquis at Mass, and a grand figure he was.
He would be carried in his sedan-chair to the
very door, and then step out as stately as
can be, with his queue tied in a fine silken
bag, his silver knee-buckles so bright you
could see yourself in them, big bows on his
shoes, and huge ruffles of the finest valenci-
ennes falling over his dainty white hands.

"'It was a brave sight,' my grandfather
said, 'to see him kneel at his *prie-dieu* with

his beautiful wife beside him. But, ah me! she drooped like a faded flower after her son disappeared. Those were sad days, they say. But Mademoiselle is very simple, and not proud at all; and when she dies there will be a Saint-Sorlin in heaven.' And so the good man talked on, for as long as one would listen."

"What a strange coincidence," thought I, "that we shall first meet on this anniversary, and thus the long prayed-for event will find its consummation!" However, on learning of the expected attendance of Mademoiselle at the Mass the next morning, we changed our plans somewhat, and went at once to see the *curé* of St. Anthony's church, to make known to him our mission, and to ask him kindly to arrange an interview for us after the Mass.

The *curé* was a simple-minded, single-hearted old man, who had for forty years served at the same altar, and who had a real affection and respect for the family De Saint-Sorlin.

The amazement, the joy of this venerable man cannot well be described at our recital. He had known the aged father of M. Savary, and with the innocent habits of thought his life had engendered he did not question our narrative, but readily believed that in my person the lost heir stood before him.

Our conversation lasted until a late hour, and I was indeed deeply impressed. It was arranged that I was to be presented to Mademoiselle the next morning at the conclusion of the Mass, when our meeting would take place in the sacristy of the church.

.   .   .   .

As we passed through the open square in front of the church at the hour appointed the next day, the spectacle was very novel that met our view. There were peasant men in their Sunday dress, and peasant women wearing their odd head-gear, built like an old-fashioned three-decker, high up, tier upon tier, and their clumsy *sabots* only half hidden by their full wide dresses. Our little party finally halted at the church door, impatient for the arrival of Mademoiselle. It was an exciting moment, as I was about to meet for the first time, on the soil of my ancestors, my sole surviving relative. And it was impossible for me to realize that I was the long prayed-for, patiently expected lost heir.

Presently the groups of peasants made respectful way for the sedan-chair, which, set upon long poles, was carefully carried by two men. The curtains were drawn, and it was not until the chair was lowered and the door opened, that I perceived a little old lady dressed in black silk, wearing a mantilla cape of the same material as her dress, and her face covered with a large black lace veil. She walked feebly, supporting herself with quite a stout cane. She did not raise her eyes or seem aware of our presence, and I followed her in respectful silence.

The *curé* had ordered that I should take the place at her side which had been for so many years vacant, but which in former times the old Marquis had occupied. It was evident that the venerable priest had not been quite able in his joy to keep his secret; for as I followed my relative slowly up the broad aisle I noticed, especially among the aged, many moist eyes.

It was indeed a solemn moment for me, and seemed too extraordinary to be possible. Here was I, an American youth and a Protestant, become the Marquis de Saint-Sorlin, and devoutly kneeling beside my Catholic cousin at a Catholic altar, the last to uphold an illustrious name. Here was I, occupying the very same place where once knelt

the haughty old Marquis, and by my very
presence confirming in the minds of all this
people the power of prayer; for had I not
been asked for, again and again, here — just
here?

So I thanked God, and begged Him to
bless those nearest and dearest to me, and to
comfort the veiled lady at my side. And
thus I prayed on, amid the solemn stillness,
as the incense rose in sweet vaporous clouds
and the silvery bell now and then was alone
heard, amid the low tones of the priest and
the gentle responses of the servers. How
poetical, how beautiful it all was!

The Mass was ended; but I remained, as
the *curé* had the evening previous requested
me to do, until I should be sent for. Mademoiselle was to be invited to come for a
moment to the sacristy when she was about
to re-enter her sedan-chair, and the good priest
said that he knew she would at once comply,

under the supposition that some work of mercy required her aid. Then my story was to be told to her, and verified by Claude and M. Savary; and when all was ready I should be sent for.

I waited one, two, three hours — it seemed to me ages; for once more my busy heart conjured new difficulties. Ah! does she refuse to recognize me? *would* force itself upon my harassed imagination. I grew faint as new complications suggested themselves. How could I now endure a fresh disappointment?

But at last the venerable *curé* entered and advanced towards me, where I still remained on my knees, as if rooted to the spot.

He whispered, "Will the Marquis de Saint-Sorlin be so good as to follow me?"

Then on bended knees he paused an instant in prayer as I worshipped beside him and gave thanks; for now I knew that all was right. In another moment the door of the sacristy was opened, and still again I knelt, to ask her blessing.

She held me at arm's length, wept, regarded me anew; then tenderly embracing me, exclaimed, —

" Now thou dost dismiss thy servant, O Lord, according to thy word in peace!"

No words can describe this affecting interview. The dear old lady had at the first announcement fainted from excess of joy, and the several hours in which I had been kept waiting had been needed in order to give her time to compose herself sufficiently for our meeting. Finally we left the sacristy, when I found the same sedan-chair, formerly used by the old Marquis, gayly decorated, and the villagers assembled and in their best attire. As I appeared with Mademoiselle leaning on my arm, shouts of joy rent the air. I placed Mademoiselle in her chair,

then entered that of my great-great-grandfather, when again cries of welcome and
shouts of " Long live the young Marquis ! "
filled the welkin.   It was a never-to-be-for-
gotten scene; and could I have had Selina
and Herbert with me, my felicity would have
been complete.   But alas! on this earth, even
when the scene is fairest, clouds must somewhat obscure the sun ; and little did I reck
the heavy anguish, the storm of grief that
even then had swept over my life.

As we proceeded on our way to the Château
de Saint-Sorlin, the good *curé* placed himself
at the head of the procession that conducted
me in triumph to my ancestral home, and
intoned a beautiful litany, the people chanting the responses of thanksgiving. As we
thus slowly ascended the hill whose summit
was crowned by the ruined castle, of which
we caught a glimpse now and then, we
passed under a garlanded arch with sacred

music and streaming banners, and thus I entered my long-lost home.

Had my wildest dreams ever pictured the reality? No; there, as I stood at the grand portal beside Mademoiselle, I thanked the people in her name and in my own for their affectionate tribute to our race, and I assured them that I would ever try to be true to the right, as were the knights of old.

. . . . . .

Claude said he was sorry that my speech could not have been repeated in the old college halls, as he thought that the President, the Faculty, Herbert, and my chums would have pronounced it first-rate.

" What are you going to do next, anyhow, old fellow ? " said Claude.

" Why ask me ? " answered I; " am I not above and beyond all, an American ? "

" Do you mean to say," said he, " that you will return to America to live ? "

" I could never for a moment entertain any other thought," I replied. " I am most thankful to know all about my name and lineage; it has in more ways than one lifted an immense weight from my heart: but all the titles, rank, and consideration the Old World could give would never induce me to forfeit my birthright, my future career as an American citizen."

" Bravo!" said Claude. " I too am of French descent; my people were of the best of the *bourgeoisie* that do honor to France. I love the nation; but I glory in being an American."

And we two college boys, for such we were as yet in heart, shook hands heartily as we congratulated ourselves on our blessed privilege.

Mademoiselle detained Claude and M. Savary as long as they would remain; but after a day spent with us they took their departure. I yielded to the entreaties of Mademoiselle, and abandoned the plan of accompanying Claude in our contemplated European tour.

It is needless to relate my prolonged conversations with my excellent relative. Hers was a beautiful nature ; nothing could exceed the generosity, the candor, the immaculate purity of her soul. Her faith seemed to me childish; but I could not refuse to admire the transparent simplicity with which she announced her sentiments. So guileless a being to have lived through a long life, I could not have imagined.

She had innumerable questions to ask of me about that past that had been shut out from her.

I narrated, not once, but twice and thrice, all that I knew about the life my great-grandfather had led in Paris, and his awful death. Then all about my dear grandfather,

— how he had moaned away his life, sighing
for the relatives he could never find; of the
short life of my father and mother; and of
my own eager desire to solve the mystery.

At every fresh incident she would utter
the most pathetic exclamations. She was so
happy that my great-great-grandfather had
intended to restore to his son the name he
had concealed, and thus deprived him of;
so happy that he died loyal to his sovereign,
— a true Saint-Sorlin! Then she wept that
he had to die; then rejoiced that he had
gained a martyr's crown for fidelity.

Finally, she begged me never to leave her.

" I am, as you see, very feeble, and I shall
be ready to depart when my dear Lord calls,
if I leave a Saint-Sorlin head of the old
house. But you must marry, Ernest; the
race must not die out."

Then she added, with charming *naïveté :*
" I always knew that Saint Anthony would

send you, or I would have married myself in my youth to preserve the race. I have looked for this day of rejoicing for fifty years. I am not surprised, Ernest, but I am thankful. And you are so like the Saint-Sorlins! The same dark-hazel eyes, aquiline nose, oval face, and the same bearing your ancestors had; only I find your hair lighter and complexion clearer than those of the other men of our family."

"Of course, dear Mademoiselle," said I, laughing, "you forget my American mother and grandmother."

"And, my son," said she, "are the natives of your land so light-colored?"

"They are as angels," I replied; for the image of Selina filled my heart.

But after a time I found courage to speak more fully. I knew it could not be long before I must undeceive her as regarded my residence in France. I felt that she had received me with the affection of a mother, and that the utmost confidence was due to her. So I forced myself to tell her the story of my love, and I avowed to her that my hopes of the future centred in America. She was much afflicted by this avowal, but after the first expression of disappointment said calmly, —

"I will pray, Ernest, for an entire submission."

After that she did not allude to the subject, except "to ask one favor," — that I should stay with her until I could receive a reply to my letter to Selina.

And this slight request I readily granted. Indeed the thought of bidding her adieu had become painful to me, and it was most interesting to be at my ancestral home.

I have not yet mentioned that on the very first night I spent at the château, wearied as I was with the intense excitements of the day, I sat up far into the hours of the early morning, scarcely permitting myself repose, that I might at once give a full account to Selina of the astounding events that had occurred. I concluded a very long letter by renewing my fervent protestations of love, and as the recognized Marquis de Saint-Sorlin, offering her the devotion of my life. And I sent through her the most affectionate messages to my dear Herbert, as well as my most respectful regards to her mother. I ended by declaring to her that the chiefest joy I experienced in the assured possession of my name and honorable descent was that I could thus meet her every wish, and place that which she coveted at her feet; and that the moment I received the favorable reply I now had every reason to hope for, I would at once return to seek my bride.

My first intention had been to go to Paris after a few days spent at the château, and make my arrangements for my return to America; but after I promised Mademoiselle to stay with her as long as possible, I wrote to my banker, asking to have any letters for me forwarded to my present address. In due time I received quite a package from America.

The first I opened was a short but loving letter from Herbert, in which he said plainly that he feared some misunderstanding had arisen between Selina and myself, and that had I given him time to do so he would have hastened to say farewell in person, although he was feeling very poorly, and in fact quite ill. This was the first time I had ever heard Herbert complain, and it made me very uneasy. Every word of this dear missive, every sentiment, was worthy of Herbert; and never before, much as I thought I loved him, had he seemed so inexpressibly dear to me. How I longed to tell him that my love for him was exceedingly great, that it in a degree surpassed that of a brother !

The next letter I opened was from Mr. King, who had evidently been hurt at my hasty departure. I felt that my unexplained movements must with good cause have seemed, to say the least, ill-considered in his eyes. He added in one line at the close of his brief communication these ominous words : " Our friend Herbert left for home to-day ; I fear that he is a very sick man."

I hastily compared the dates, and found that Mr. King's letter had been written three days later than Herbert's, which must have been left at the lawyer's office; and sent with his mail in the same steamer. Mechanically I picked up several papers, glanced at them, for my thoughts were far away, and finally took a magazine out of the packet. Instantly underneath this magazine, and exposed to view by its removal, I noticed a large letter with a black seal.

It was strange that it could, even for a moment, have escaped my attention. The superscription was in the delicate tracery of Selina's hand. I knew before I opened the envelope that it meant disaster. But how unprepared was I for the full nature of its contents, which, like the tangled threads that form the warp and woof of life, were of both joy and sorrow!

Selina wrote : —

MY BELOVED ERNEST, — We are crushed to the earth; our Herbert is no more! How can I find the strength to tell you, his best beloved friend, of our terrible loss! But oh, Ernest, I deserved to pass under this chastening rod, for I was filled with sinful pride, — pride of race and pride on his account! In my eyes he was as a fixed star of the first magnitude, and no glory was too great for him. At times a horrible fear overwhelms me that I may have urged him to over-exertion in my insane ambition for him.

Ambition! I now loathe the very word. Can it bring back our dead? Ah me, we are bereft!

All things seemed alike easy to him, possible for him; and I never could realize that accomplishment cost him effort. But I need not tell *you*, Ernest, what he was, or all that he was; for were you not, of all others, the one chosen friend whom he loved?

He came home to us, arriving very unexpectedly, and at the first moment we embraced him overjoyed; but at the next glance we saw how ill and haggard he looked.

Ernest, he came home to die!

Must I write on? Poor mother! it must kill her; she cannot live long under this consuming grief. Oh, our broken hearts! Ernest, pity our anguish! Our Herbert died of a congestion of the brain; Mr. King thinks that he worked too hard. This kind gentleman often begged him to take some repose, and not sit up at night writing those brilliant magazine articles and beautiful poems after giving so many hours to the study of law; the strain was too great.

And what adds to mother's anguish is that he wrote so much that he might send cheques to her.   You know we are not rich, Ernest, and Herbert was so anxious to surround mother with all the luxuries of the olden days.   Once he wrote: " Mother, here is a cheque for my last article.   Why not now drive, as you once did, in your carriage?   You see I already can procure your former comforts for you.   They may be luxuries to others, but they are necessities for you, mother mine."   Was there ever such a dear, generous heart?

How can I tell you the rest, Ernest?   At first he seemed only very weak, and tottered as he walked.   It wrung our hearts when we thought of that elastic bound, that light and buoyant step we used to hear, like music about the house.   Then he could not sleep.   Oh, the terrible prolonged insomnia!

" Mother," he would say, " billions upon billions of thoughts rush over me and overpower me, like ocean-breakers!   I grapple with an army of them, only to meet the advancing hosts; higher, still higher, they roll!   Some are foam-crested, some have gorgon-heads, some are sea-sirens; and others are innumerable angels' wings that beat down the sea-monsters."

Mother said to the Doctor: " Is this delirium, Doctor, he seems so calm?"

The physician shook his head and said: " Time and rest and Nature; let us hope in absolute rest, madam."

Then again Herbert said: " Mother, the Mississippi River tries to find an outlet through my brain, and the pressure is killing me." This was after a long, wakeful night.

At times he would seem to revive and be himself once more. On one of these occasions he asked me why I sent you away. I dared not deceive him, or keep back from him anything in his then state, and I told him all.

He was greatly distressed, and repeated several times, as if to himself: " Dear Ernest, noblehearted Ernest!" Then, turning to me with the most displeased look I had ever seen him wear, he said: " Selina, you were very foolish, unkind, and unjust. You have overlooked the true worth of one of the best of men. You have brought unhappiness upon us all for a mere bauble."

" Oh, Herbert," I replied, " did I not learn the lesson from you to be proud of our race, proud of our name?"

"Yes, Selina. A just pride in the record of one's ancestors is an incentive to strive for excellence; but what in the dead past can for a moment compare to that nobility which is innate? When you found that God had given the patent, why ask more?"

"I see, my Herbert," I replied; "our Ernest is one of Nature's noblemen."

He smiled, and said: "Write him all this; tell him we are content with the name he bears, and we are sure that he will win whatever recognition he wishes. Tell him that we all love him; we three are one in this. I know I may speak for mother."

Soon after this conversation, Ernest, which was really Herbert's last message to you, he grew rapidly weaker, and after some days did not rise from his bed. One morning mother entered his room, and found him with a flushed face and a certain light in his eyes she had never before noticed.

I must not forget to tell you, Ernest, that by some strange fatality Herbert died in our chamber of sorrow. He asked for it when he first arrived, and mother did not like to refuse him. Could he have had a premonition that he had come home to die? Mother took a small room opening into this desolate chamber, from whence she could watch over him at night, and usually the door was left open between the apartments. She would beg Herbert to speak to her if he were awake, although he never would disturb her. But on the night preceding this particular morning he had asked to have the door closed, and to be left quite in the dark. So when mother entered he said:

"Mother, I have had a vision!"

"A vision, my son!" she exclaimed in astonishment; "you mean a dream."

"No, mother, not a dream, but, as I tell you, a vision. After you left me in utter darkness, as usual, I could not sleep. I lay awake feeling calm and praying God to be resigned, when suddenly the room filled with light. I call it 'light,' because as yet I have no other word whereby to express such transcendent brightness as encompassed me. Amid this great glory there shone a majestic figure surmounting a dome of brilliancy like a mountain ablaze. Millions of angels' heads bowed before this dazzling effulgence, and I felt my soul convulsed with pangs as of dissolution striving to mount to its primal source. Mother mine, be not dismayed, but this vision means life eternal."

My mother sank upon her knees, and tried for his sake to repress her agony, as his eyes closed with a tired look.

After this he grew rapidly worse, and lived only a few days. He was most of the time unconscious. Once he opened his eyes wide, and called with a loud voice and an eager look, "Father!" Did our father come to conduct his well-beloved son on the lonely way? Then again he cried out, "Selina! Ernest!" and just an instant before he breathed his last breath he said, with the most pathetic tone, "Mother!" and with this dear word on his lips, expired.

Ernest, I feel that mother cannot long survive this fatal blow. Our home is indeed a crumbling ruin, and totters to its decline; for the keystone of the arch has fallen, and most sorrowful is the heart of

SELINA SHIRLEY.

Herbert dead! Selina mine! How could I endure at one and the same instant such excess of grief and such longed-for happiness? But no; my soul at this moment can only comprehend its desolation. For is not sorrow a deeper feeling, one more closely interwoven with man's destiny in this valley of tears, than joy?

Oh, my Herbert, my beloved brother, twin of my soul, how fondly had I looked forward to thy companionship? What dreams had I not cherished of the delight attendant upon making it easier for thee to climb Fame's ladder, for I well knew thou must ever rise high and higher! But ah, all too gross for thy beautiful nature would have been that harvest which is reaped of earth's fruition! When thine eyes beheld the translucent brightness of another world, thy soul was convulsed with pangs unto dissolution in thy intense desire to mount to that highest plane! And now that thou hast ascended to the skies, why wish to call thee back?

A sacred trust is mine! Thy mother shall become my mother; thy sister my wife; and

I will, while ever deploring thy loss and uniting my tears with theirs, try, so far as can be, to take the place made vacant. I must make all haste to support the falling arch; I can see Selina standing therein, and hear her gentle voice calling upon me to save them.

As soon as the violence of my grief would permit, I made known my loss to my dear relative. She who had always led so lonely a life knew well how to comfort the sorrowful, and she who had always been so unselfish knew how to make sacrifices. Forgetful of herself, she bade me God-speed, and counselled me to leave at once, in order to assume the sacred trust confided to my tender care. And she added, with sadness in her voice:

" I fear we shall never meet again. The broken hearted mother must be lovingly cared for, and you must now take Herbert's place at her side. I had hoped," — and here

she brushed away the unbidden tears, —
" indeed, I had cherished a dream of your
return with your beautiful bride (who, thank
Heaven ! is descended from a brave and noble
race), and a vision of fair children making
glad this desolate old castle. Yet even if I
am no more, I pray you, Ernest, when the
mother has joined her son, come back, at
least for a time. Do not, I beg you, forever abandon your ancestral halls. And
promise me one thing more, — when in his
own time the dear Lord sends you a daughter, let her bear the honored name that the
women of our race have borne since the
gentle Estelle drooped and died, sorrowing
for her son, — the name that son, your great-
great-grandfather, still loved, even in the fury
of his utmost wrath : let the child be called
Estelle Desmarets."

" Cousin Estelle," I replied, " if God so
bless me in the future, I promise it."

That night I bade her a sad and affectionate farewell. I had learned to love her, and
I wept with her as I knelt to kiss her hands
and receive her blessing. As the sun rose
the next morning I stood beside my saddled
horse on the ramparts of the Château de
Saint-Sorlin. Yet I would fain for one moment more view anew the fair scene which
for centuries had been so intimately connected with the destinies of my people.

The castle was an irregular structure and
most picturesque in its partial decay, for as
it had not been repaired for half a century,
the ravages of time had defaced the structure. Once it had been surrounded by fine
gardens, of which only some vestiges remained; but the terrace-walks were shaded
by splendid chestnut and poplar trees. In
former times it had frowned from its rugged
height as a fortified place, and its now grass-
grown ramparts and moss-covered bulwarks

rested on jagged rocks. As I paused for one last look, the roseate dawn tipped with jewelled fingers these immense crags and the castle's gray, vine-clad walls, gilded its turrets, glided along its parapets, lighted up the crannies of its loopholes, and enwreathed as with an aureole its engraven escutcheon. Glimpses of dreamy dells were opened to view, and the silver line of sinuous streams diversified the landscape with their living tracery, while in the plain below glowed the picturesque and quaint hamlet. Suddenly a broad flood of flame shot forth from the new-born sun and transfigured the snow-clad peaks of Mont Blanc in the far distance.

"Thank God!" thought I. "The house of my forefathers goes not down unto the tomb of oblivion. I accept the propitious writing in the sky, the pleasing omen of a newly-risen sun!"

.   .   .   .   .   .

A score of years have sped onward! They have brought both joy and sorrow in their course. Herbert's broken-hearted mother did not long survive his loss, but she lived to welcome and to bless the fair-haired Herbert, our first-born. Thus Selina had herself a mother's cares when we lost Mrs. Shirley. And during all these years dear Mr. King has always been our chosen friend, — he and Claude, whom we often entertain as our guests.

A decade of the score of years had passed by, and once more the simple villagers of Nuits de Saint-Sorlin assembled with music and banners to receive us, — this time the dear old *curé* no longer at their head, for he was chanting his litanies in heaven. But our saintly cousin was still living when I took to her Selina and the three cherubs, who made the old halls ring again with their joyous clamor. And she grew young again with Herbert, Ernest, and Estelle at her knees. The dear Lord in whom she ever trusted with such a childlike confidence had spared her for this gladdened old age. In every way we sought to please her. I lavished of my abundance to help her poor and to repair the old castle. We did not leave her again, but tried to encompass her declining days with the fulness of our affection.

And now the wonderful dream that I dreamed when I spent that first night in the haunted chamber had been verified. Let us recall its scenes and their fulfilment.

Herbert died; his soul took its flight heavenward from that very bed. My cries of despair were silenced by faith and prayer. Then Providence, taking in hand the helm of my destiny, caused me to cross the ocean, where my name of Saint-Sorlin was restored to me, and through it happiness was regained. Finally our fledglings, the trio of cherubs' heads, were sent to support the falling arch. All this has become a part of our family tradition.

When in the course of years our venerated cousin Estelle closed her eyes on earth to open them again in heaven, then we took our flight back to our native land. At last, a man midway in life, wearied with repose, I yield to my instincts, and with the full fever of my American blood coursing in my veins, plunge into business.

First and best, I love my native country, America, and I meet the inexorable fate of its men. I have become matter-of-fact. I have embraced a profession. I am in league with the great power of this nation. My whole life is now devoted to romancing, but in a business way; for, dear reader, I am a journalist.

A LIST OF BOOKS

PUBLISHED BY

TICKNOR AND COMPANY

BOSTON.

AMERICAN–ACTOR SERIES (THE). Edited by LAU-
RENCE HUTTON. A series of 12mo volumes by the best writers, embracing
the lives of the most famous and popular American Actors. Illustrated.
Six volumes in three. Sold only in sets. Per set, $5.00.

    Vol. I. Edwin Forrest. By Lawrence Barrett. The Jeffersons. By
    William Winter.
    Vol. II. The Elder and the Younger Booth. By Mrs. Asia Booth Clarke.
    Charlotte Cushman. By Clara Erskine Clement.
    Vol. III. Mrs. Duff. By Joseph N. Ireland. Fechter. By Kate Field.
    Also a limited edition on large paper, especially adapted to the use of
    collectors and bibliophiles, for extending, extra illustrating, etc. 6 vols.
    Per vol., $5.00.

AMERICAN ARCHITECT. See last page.

ARCHITECTURE. See MONOGRAPH.

ARNOLD'S (EDWIN) The Light of Asia. Beautiful illustrated edition. 8vo. $6.00. In antique morocco, or tree-calf, $10.00.

ARNOLD'S (GEORGE) Poems. Edited, with a Biographi-
cal Sketch of the Poet, by WILLIAM WINTER. With Portrait. 16mo. $1.50.
Half-calf, $3.00. Morocco antique or tree-calf, $4.00.

AUSTIN'S (JANE G.) Nantucket Scraps ; Being Experiences of an Off-Islander, in Season and out of Season, among a Passing
People. 16mo. $1.50.

BACON'S (HENRY) Parisian Art and Artists. 8vo. Profusely illustrated. $3.00.

BALLOU'S (MATURIN M.) Edge-Tools of Speech. 1 vol. 8vo. $3.50; sheep, $5.00; half-calf or half-morocco, $6.50.

BARTLETT'S (TRUMAN H.) The Art-Life of William Rimmer. With Illustrations after his Paintings, Drawings, and Sculptures. 4to. Full gilt. $10.00.

BELLAMY'S (EDWARD) Miss Ludington's Sister. $1.25.

BENT'S (SAMUEL ARTHUR) Short Sayings of Great Men. 8vo. Third edition. $3.00. Half-calf, $5.50.

BOIT'S (ROBERT APTHORP) Eustis. 12mo. $1.50.

BOSTON, Memorial History of. See page 22.

BOWDOIN COLLEGE. See CLEAVELAND.

BROOKS'S (HENRY M.) Olden-Time Series. Each vol. 16mo. 50 cents.
    I.   Curiosities of the Old Lottery.
    II. Days of The Spinning-Wheel in New England.
    III. New-England Sunday.
Other volumes in preparation.

BROWN'S (FRANCES CLIFFORD) A Stroll with Keats. 1 vol. Square 16mo. Richly illustrated. $1.50.

BROWN'S (HELEN DAWES) Two College Girls. 12mo. $1.50.

BROWN'S (SUSAN ANNA) The Invalid's Tea-Tray. Illuminated boards. 50 cents.

——————— How the Ends Met. 12mo. 50 cents.

——————— In Bridget's Vacation. Leaflets to hang up. 50 cents. On gilt bar and rings. 75 cents.

BUDDHIST RECORDS OF THE WESTERN WORLD. Translated from the original Chinese, with Introduction, Index, etc. By SAMUEL BEAL, Trinity College, Cambridge. 2 vols. 12mo. $7.00.

BUDGE'S (ERNEST A.) The History of Esarhaddon (Son of Sennacherib), King of Assyria, B.C. 681-668. From Cuneiform Inscriptions. 8vo. Gilt top. $4.00.

BUNNER'S (H. C.) A Woman of Honor. 16mo. $1.25.

BUSH'S (JAMES S.) The Evidence of Faith. 12mo. $2.00.

BYRON'S (LORD) Childe Harold. A sumptuous new illustrated edition. In box. $6.00. In antique morocco, or tree-calf, $10.00. In crushed Levant, with silk linings, $25.00.
    The great holiday book of 1885-1886.

CABLE'S (GEORGE W.) Doctor Sevier. 12mo. $1.50.

CARLYLE (Thomas) and *RALPH WALDO EMER-SON*, The Correspondence of. Edited by Charles Eliot Norton. 2 vols. 12mo. Gilt tops and rough edges. With new Portraits. $4.00. Half-calf, $8.00. Half-morocco, gilt top, uncut edges, $8.00.
New revised edition with 100 pages of newly-found letters.

———— Supplementary Volume, including the newly-found letters. 16mo. $1.00.

CAROLINO'S (Pedro) New Guide of the Conversation in Portuguese and English. First American edition. With an Introduction by Mark Twain. 16mo. $1.00. Paper, 50 cents.

CARRYL'S (Charles E.) Davy and the Goblin. 1 vol. 8vo. Fully illustrated. $1.50.

CESNOLA'S (Gen. L. P. di) The Cesnola Collection of Cyprus Antiquities. A Descriptive and Pictorial Atlas. Large folio. 500 Plates. *Sold by subscription only.* Send for Prospectus.

CHAMBERLAIN'S (Basil Hall) The Classical Poetry of the Japanese. 8vo. $3.00.

CHASE'S (Miss E. B.) Over the Border. 1 vol. 12mo. Illustrated with Heliotype Engravings from Original Drawings of Scenery in Nova Scotia. With Map. 12mo. Third edition. $1.50.

CHENOWETH'S (Mrs. C. van D.) Stories of the Saints. Illustrated. 12mo. $2.00.

CLARK'S (T. M.) Building Superintendence. 8vo. With Plans, etc. $3.00.

CLARKE'S (Rev. James Freeman) Every-Day Religion. 1 vol. 12mo. $1.50.

———— Events and Epochs in Religious History. Crown 8vo. Illustrated. $3.00. Half-calf, $5.50.

———— The Ideas of the Apostle Paul. 12mo. $1.50.

———— Self-Culture. Eleventh edition. 12mo. $1.50. Half-calf, $3.00.

CLEAVELAND'S (Nehemiah) and *PACKARD'S* (Alpheus Spring) History of Bowdoin College. With Biographical Sketches of its Graduates, from 1806 to 1879, inclusive. With many full-page Portraits, and other Illustrations. 8vo. $5.00.

CLEMENT'S (Clara Erskine) and Laurence Hutton's Artists of the Nineteenth Century. 12mo. Fully revised up to 1885. $3.00. Half-calf, $5.00. Tree-calf, $7.00.

———— A Handbook of Legendary and Mythological Art. Eighteenth edition. 12mo. $3. Half-calf, $5. Tree-calf, $7.

———— Painters, Sculptors, Architects, Engravers, and their Works. Illustrated profusely. Ninth edition. 12mo. $3.00. Half-calf, $5.00. Tree-calf, $7.00.

———— Eleanor Maitland. A Novel. 16mo. $1.25.

CLEMMER'S (MARY) Poems of Life and Nature. $1.50.

COLLIER'S (ROBERT LAIRD) English Home Life. 16mo.
Gilt top. $1.00.

COLLING'S (J. K.) Art Foliage. Entirely new plates
from the latest enlarged London edition. Folio. $10.00.

CONWAY'S (M. D.) Emerson at Home and Abroad. $1.50.

COOKE'S (GEORGE WILLIS) George Eliot ; A Critical
Study of her Life, Writings, and Philosophy. 12mo. With Portrait. $2.00.
Half-calf, $4.00.

———— Ralph Waldo Emerson ; His Life, Writings, and
Philosophy. 12mo. With Portrait. $2.00. Half-calf, $4.00.

———— (MRS. LAURA S. H.) Dimple Dopp. Small
4to. Illustrated. $1.25.

———— (ROSE TERRY) Somebody's Neighbors. 12mo.
Fourth edition. $1.50. Half-calf, $3.00.

———— The Sphinx's Children. 12mo. $1.50.

CRADDOCK'S (CHARLES EGBERT) Where the Battle
Was Fought. A Novel. 12mo. Fourth edition. $1.50.

CUNNINGHAM'S (FRANK H.) Familiar Sketches of the
Phillips Exeter Academy and Surroundings. Illustrated. $2.50.

DAHLGREN'S (MRS. MADELEINE VINTON) A Washington
Winter. 12mo. $1.50.

———————————— Memoir of John A. Dahlgren, Rear-Admiral
U. S. Navy. 8vo. With Portrait and Illustrations. $3.00.

———————————— South-Sea Sketches. 12mo. $1.50.

———————————— South-Mountain Magic. 12mo. $1.50.

DAMEN'S GHOST. Vol. VI. of the Round-Robin Series
of novels. 16mo. $1.00. In paper covers, 50 cents.

DANENHOWER'S (LIEUT. J. W.) Narrative of the
Jeannette. Paper covers. 25 cents.

DESMOND HUNDRED (THE). Vol. XI. of the Round-
Robin Series of novels. $1.00. In paper covers, 50 cents.

DOBSON'S (AUSTIN) Thomas Bewick and his Pupils.
With numerous Illustrations. Crown 8vo. $3.50. Limited large-paper
edition. $10.00.

DOCTOR BEN. Vol. XIII. of the Round-Robin Series of
novels. $1.00. In paper covers, 50 cents.

DODGE'S (THEODORE AYRAULT, U.S.A.) A Bird's-Eye
View of our Civil War. 1 vol. 8vo. With Maps and Illustrations. $3.00

———— The Campaign of Chancellorsville. 8vo. $3.00.

DOROTHEA. Vol. X. of the Round-Robin Series of
novels. 16mo $1.00. In paper covers, 50 cents.

DU MAURIER'S (GEORGE) Pictures from Society. 50
full-page Pictures from *Punch.* 1 vol. 4to. Full gilt. $5.00.

EASTWICK'S (EDWARD B., F.R.S., M.R.A.S.) The Gulistan; or, Rose Garden of Shekh Mushlin'ddin Sâdî. 8vo. $3.50.

EATON'S (D. CADY) Handbook of Greek and Roman
Sculpture. Second edition, revised and enlarged. 12mo. $2.00.

EDMUNDSON'S (GEORGE) Milton and Vondel. A Curiosity of Literature. 1 vol. Crown 8vo. $2.50.

EMERSON, The Genius and Character of. A Series of
Lectures delivered at the Concord School of Philosophy, by eminent authors and critics. Edited by F. B. SANBORN. Illustrated. 12mo. $2.00.

EMERSON-CARLYLE CORRESPONDENCE (THE).
See CARLYLE.

EMERSON'S (MRS. ELLEN RUSSELL) Myths of the Indians; or, Legends, Traditions, and Symbols of the Aborigines of America. 8vo. Gilt top. With numerous Plates and Diagrams. $5.00.

FANCHETTE. Vol. XV. of the Round-Robin Series of
novels. $1.00. In paper covers, 50 cents.

FAVORITE-AUTHORS SERIES. Favorite Authors,
Household Friends, Good Company. Three volumes in one. Illustrated. 8vo. Full gilt. $3.50.

FAWCETT'S (EDGAR) Social Silhouettes. 12mo. $1.50.
——————— The Adventures of a Widow. 12mo. $1.50.
——————— Tinkling Cymbals. A Novel. 12mo. $1.50.
——————— Song and Story. A volume of Poems. $1.50.

FEATHERMAN'S (A.) The Aramæans; Social History
of the Races of Mankind. 8vo. Uncut edges, gilt top. $5.00.

FENOLLOSA'S (ERNEST F.) Review of the Chapter on
Painting in Gonse's "L'Art Japonais." 12mo. Paper covers. 25 cents.

FOOTE'S (MRS. MARY HALLOCK) The Led-Horse Claim.
A Novel. Illustrated by the Author. 16mo. $1.25.

FROMENTIN (EUGÈNE): Painter and Writer. From the
French of Louis Gonse, by Mrs. MARY C. ROBBINS. 8vo. Illustrated. $3.00.

FROMENTIN'S (EUGÈNE) The Old Masters of Belgium
and Holland. 8vo. With eight full-page Heliotypes. Translated by Mrs. MARY C. ROBBINS. $3.00.

FULLER'S (ALBERT W.) Artistic Homes in City and
Country. Fourth edition. Oblong folio. 76 full-page Illustrations. $4.50.

GARDNER'S (E. C.) Homes and all about them. 3 vols.
in 1. Profusely illustrated. 12mo. $2.50.

GARFIELD (PRESIDENT JAMES ABRAM) The Works of.
Edited by BURKE A. HINSDALE. 2 vols. 8vo. With new Steel Portraits. $6.00. Sheep, $8.50. Half-morocco or half-calf, $10.00.
Edition de luxe. 2 vols. 8vo. $25.00. *Sold by subscription only.*

GAYARRE'S (Charles) Aubert Dubayet. 12mo. $2.00.

GEORGIANS (The). Vol. III. of the Round-Robin Series of novels. 16mo. $1.00. In paper covers, 50 cents.

GERALDINE: A Souvenir of the St. Lawrence. A Poetical Romance. 16mo. Seventh edition. $1.25. Half-calf, $3.00.

GOETHE, The Life and Genius of. Concord Lectures for 1885. Edited by F. B. Sanborn and W. T. Harris. With Portraits. $2.00.

GOETHE'S Faust. Translated by A. Hayward. $1.25.

GRANT'S (Robert) An Average Man. 12mo. $1.50.

——— The Confessions of a Frivolous Girl. $1.25.

· ——— The Knave of Hearts. $1.25.

GREENOUGH'S (Mrs. R.) Mary Magdalene. $1.50.

GRÉVILLE'S (Henry) Cleopatra. A Russian Romance. 1 vol. 16mo. With portrait of the author. $1.25.

——— Dosia's Daughter. Translated by Mrs. Clara Erskine Clement. $1.25.

HALE'S (Lucretia P.) The Peterkin Papers. 16mo. $1.00.

HAMLIN'S (Augustus C.) Leisure Hours among the Gems. Illustrated. 12mo. $2.00.

HARRIS'S (Joel Chandler) Mingo, and other Sketches in Black and White. 16mo. $1.25.

——— Nights with Uncle Remus. Illustrated. $1.50.

HARTING'S (James Edmund, F.L.S., F.Z.S.) British Animals Extinct within Historic Times. With some Account of British Wild White Cattle. Illustrated. 8vo. Gilt top. $4.50.

HARTT'S (Professor C. F.) Geology and Physical Geography of Brazil. *In preparation.*

HASSARD'S (J. R. G.) A Pickwickian Pilgrimage. 16mo. $1.00.

HATTON'S (Joseph) Henry Irving's Impressions of America. 1 vol. 12mo. $1.50.

HAWTHORNE'S (Julian) Nathaniel Hawthorne and his Wife. A Biography. With New Portraits on Steel, and Etched Vignettes. 2 vols. 12mo. $5.00. Half-morocco or half-calf, $9.00. Edition de luxe. $12.00.

——— Love — or a Name. 12mo. $1.50.

——— Beatrix Randolph. 12mo. $1.50.

——— Fortune's Fool. 12mo. $1.50.

HAWTHORNE'S (Nathaniel) Dr. Grimshawe's Secret. 12mo. $1.50. Library edition. Gilt top. $2.00.

HAYES'S (Henry) The Story of Margaret Kent. $1.50.

HAYWARD'S (ALMIRA L.) The Illustrated Birthday
Book of American Poets. Revised and enlarged edition, with index for
names, and portraits of thirteen great American poets. 1 vol. 18mo. $1.00.
Half-calf, $2.25. Flexible morocco, seal or calf, $3.00.

HAZEN'S (GEN. W. B.) A Narrative of Military Service.
8vo. With Maps, Plans, and Illustrations. $3.00.

HEARN'S (LAFCADIO) Stray Leaves from Strange Litera-
ture. Stories reconstructed from the Anvari-Soheili, Baital-Pachisi, Ma-
habharata, Gulistan, etc. 1 vol. 16mo. $1.50.

HENDERSON'S (ISAAC). The Prelate. A Novel. 1 vol.
12mo. With covers designed by Elihu Vedder. $1.50.

HINSDALE'S (BURKE A.) President Garfield and Educa-
tion. Portraits of Gen. Garfield, Mrs. Garfield, etc. 12mo. $1.50. Half-
calf, $3.00. Morocco antique, $4.00.

———————— Schools and Studies. 16mo. $1.50.

HIS SECOND CAMPAIGN. Vol. XVI. of the Round-
Robin Series of novels. 16mo. $1.00. In paper covers, 50 cents.

HOME-BOOK OF ART (THE). Heliotype Plates after
One Hundred Classical and Popular Pictures by the most famous Artists of
the World. With descriptions. Twenty-five parts at one dollar each. Or
all bound in 1 vol. Cloth, $28.00. Half morocco, $31.00. Full morocco,
$33.00. *By subscription only.*

HOMOSELLE. Vol. V. of the Round-Robin Series of
novels. 16mo. $1.00. In paper covers, 50 cents.

HOSMER'S (G. W.) The People and Politics. 8vo. $3.00.

HOWARD'S (BLANCHE W.) Aulnay Tower. 12mo. $1.50.

———————— Aunt Serena. A Novel. 16mo. Thirteenth
edition. $1.25.

———————— Guenn. 12mo. Fifth edition. $1.50.

HOWE'S (E. W.) The Mystery of the Locks. 12mo. $1.50.

———————— The Story of a Country Town. 12mo. Fourth
edition. $1.50.

HOWELLS'S (W. D.) Tuscan Cities. With many fine
Illustrations, by JOSEPH PENNELL. Richly bound, full gilt edges, in box,
$5.00. In tree-calf, or antique morocco, $10.00.

———————— Indian Summer. 12mo. $1.50.

———————— The Rise of Silas Lapham. 12mo. $1.50.

———————— A Fearful Responsibility. 12mo. $1.50.

———————— A Modern Instance. 12mo. $1.50.

———————— A Woman's Reason. 12mo. $1.50.

———————— Dr. Breen's Practice. 12mo. $1.50.

HOWELLS'S (W. D.) The Elevator. 32mo. 50 cents.

———————— The Sleeping-Car. 32mo. 50 cents.

———————— The Parlor Car. 32mo. 50 cents.

———————— The Register. 32mo. 50 cents.

———————— Three Villages. Little-Classic size. $1.25.

———————— Poems. New revised edition. 1 vol. 12mo.
In box. Printed on fine hand-made paper. Parchment covers. $2.00.

———————— A Counterfeit Presentment. A Comedy.
Little-Classic size. $1.25.

———————— Out of the Question. A Comedy. Little-
Classic size. $1.25.

———————— A Little Girl among the Old Masters. Being
her own Compositions and Inventions in Sacred and Legendary Art. With
Introduction and Commentary by W. D. Howells. Oblong. Fifty-four
Illustrations. $2.00.

———————— Choice Autobiographies. A collection of the
most entertaining autobiographies, carefully edited, and with preliminary
Critical and Biographical Essays. Little-Classic size. 8 vols. Each, $1.25.

　　I., II.　Memoirs of Frederica Sophia Wilhelmina, Margravine
　　　　　　of Baireuth.
　　III.　Lord Herbert of Cherbury, and Thomas Ellwood.
　　IV.　Vittorio Alfieri.
　　V.　Carlo Goldoni.
　　VI.　Edward Gibbon.
　　VII., VIII.　François Marmontel.

HUBBARD'S (Lucius L.) Woods and Lakes of Maine.
A Trip from Moosehead Lake to New Brunswick in a Birch-Bark Canoe.
With Indian place-names and their meanings. 1 vol. 8vo. With Illustrations, and a large map. $3.00. Half-calf, $5.50. Tree-calf, or antique
morocco, $8.00.

HUNNEWELL'S (James F.) The Historical Monuments
of France. 1 vol. 8vo. Illustrated. $3.50.

———————— Bibliography of Charlestown, Mass., and
Bunker Hill. 1 vol. 8vo. Illustrated. $2.00.

HUTCHINSON'S (Ellen M.) Songs and Lyrics. 16mo.
With Frontispiece. $1.25.

HUTTON'S (Laurence) Literary Landmarks of London.
1 vol. 12mo. $1.50.

IRVING (Henry). See Hatton.

JAMES (Henry, Sr.), The Literary Remains of. Edited by William James. 1 vol. 12mo. With Portrait. $2.00.

JAMES'S (Henry) The Author of Beltraffio ; Pandora ;
Georgina's Reasons ; The Path of Duty ; Four Meetings. 12mo. $1.50.

———————— The Siege of London ; The Pension Beaurepas ;
and The Point of View. 12mo. $1.50.

JAMES'S (HENRY) Tales of Three Cities (The Impressions
of a Cousin; Lady Barberina; A New-England Winter). 12mo. $1.50.

———— A Little Tour in France. 12mo. $1.50.

———— Portraits of Places. 12mo. $1.50.

———— Daisy Miller : A Comedy. 12mo. $1.50.

JOHNSON'S (ROSSITER) Idler and Poet. 16mo. $1.25.

JOHNSTON'S (ELIZABETH BRYANT) Original Portraits
of Washington. Sixty Portraits, from paintings, sculptures, etc. With
descriptive text. 1 vol. 4to. $15.00. Half morocco, $20.00. *By subscription only.*

KEENE'S (CHARLES) Our People. Four Hundred Pictures from *Punch.* 4to. $5.00.

KENDRICK'S (PROFESSOR A. C.) Our Poetical Favorites.
Three volumes in one. Illustrated. 8vo. Full gilt. $3.50.

KING'S (CLARENCE) Mountaineering in the Sierra Nevada.
12mo. With Maps. Eighth edition. $2.00.

KING'S (EDWARD) The Golden Spike. 12mo. $1.50.

———— The Gentle Savage. 12mo. $2.00.

KIRK'S (MRS. ELLEN OLNEY) A Midsummer Madness.
A Novel. 1 vol. 16mo. $1.25.

LEONE. Vol. XII. of the Round-Robin Series of novels.
16mo. $1.00. In paper covers, 50 cents.

LEOPARDI'S (G.) Essays and Dialogues. 8vo. $3.00.

LESSON IN LOVE (A). Vol. II. of the Round-Robin
Series of novels. 16mo. $1.00. In paper covers, 50 cents.

LIEBER, The Life and Letters of Francis. Edited by
Thomas Sergeant Perry. 8vo. With Portrait. $3.00. Half-calf, $5.50.

LIGHT ON THE HIDDEN WAY. With Introduction
by JAMES FREEMAN CLARKE. 1 vol. 16mo. $1.00.

LINCOLN'S (MRS. JEANIE GOULD) Her Washington
Season. A Novel. 12mo. $1.50.

LONGFELLOW'S (SAMUEL) Life of Henry Wadsworth
Longfellow. With extracts from his Journals and Correspondence. Crown
8vo 2 vols. With Steel Portraits, Engravings on wood, fac-similies, etc.
$6.00; half-calf, with marbled edges, $11.00; half-morocco, with gilt top
and rough edges, $11.00.
* *Also, Edition de Luxe, with Proof Portraits.*

LOWELL'S (PERCIVAL) Chosön: The Land of the Morning Calm. A Sketch of Korea. 1 vol. 8vo. Illustrated. $5.00.

MACHIAVELLI (NICCOLO), The Historical, Political,
and Diplomatic Works of. Translated by Christian E. Detmold. 4 vols.
8vo, with Steel Frontispieces, in a box. $15. Half-calf, $30.

MADAME LUCAS. Vol. VIII. of the Round-Robin Series of novels. 16mo. $1.00. In paper covers, 50 cents.

MADDEN'S (F. W.) The Coins of the Jews. 4to. $12.00.

MEREDITH'S (OWEN) Lucile, Illustrated. Holiday Edition. With 160 new Illustrations. Elegantly bound, with full gilt edges, in box, $6.00. Tree-calf or antique morocco, $10.00. Calf or morocco, inlaid mosaic, $12.50. Crushed levant, silk linings, $25.00.

———————— Lucile. Tremont Edition. 1 vol. 16mo. Beautifully illustrated. With red lines and gilt edges, $2.50. Half-calf, $4.00. Antique morocco, tree-calf, flexible calf, or seal, $6.00.

———————— Lucile. Pocket Edition. 1 vol. Little-Classic size. Thirty Illustrations. Elegantly bound, $1.00. Half-calf, $2.25. Antique morocco, flexible calf, or seal, $3.00. Tree-calf, $3.50.

MONOGRAPHS OF AMERICAN ARCHITECTURE, No. 1. Harvard Law School. H. H. Richardson, architect. 18 Plates (Gelatine, from nature), 13 × 16. In portfolio. $5.00. No. 2. The State Capitol, at Hartford, Conn., Richard M. Upjohn, architect. 22 Plates (Gelatine, from nature), 13 × 16. $6.00.

MORSE'S (EDWARD S., PH.D.) Japanese Homes and their Surroundings. 8vo. With 300 Illustrations. $5.00; half-calf, $9.00.

NAMELESS NOBLEMAN (A). Vol. I. of the Round-Robin Series of novels. 16mo. $1.00. In paper covers, 50 cents.

NELSON'S (HENRY L.) John Rantoul. 12mo. $1.50.

NORTON'S (GEN. C. B.) American Inventions in Breech-loading Small Arms, Heavy Ordnance, etc. 4to. 250 Engravings. $10.00.

OWEN'S (WILLIAM MILLER) In Camp and Battle with the Washington Artillery of New Orleans. Illustrated with Maps and Engravings. 1 vol. 8vo. $3.00.

PALFREY'S (JOHN GORHAM) A Compendious History of New England. 4 vols. 12mo. With new Index. In a box. $6.00. Half-calf, $12.00.

PATTY'S PERVERSITIES. Vol. IV. of the Round-Robin Series of novels. 16mo. $1.00. In paper covers, 50 cents.

PEIRCE'S (MRS. MELUSINA FAY) Co-operative House-keeping. Square 16mo. 60 cents.

PENINSULAR CAMPAIGN (THE) of General McClellan in 1862. (Vol. I., Papers of the Military Historical Society of Massachusetts.) 8vo. With Maps. $3.00.

PERRY'S (NORA) For a Woman. 16mo. $1.00.

———————— A Book of Love Stories. 16mo. $1.00.

PERRY'S (THOMAS SERGEANT) From Opitz to Lessing. 1 vol. 16mo. $1.25.

PICTURESQUE SKETCHES. Statues, Monuments, Fountains, Cathedrals, Towers, etc. 1 vol. Oblong folio. $1.50.

PLYMPTON'S (Miss A. G.) The Glad Year Round.
Square 8vo. $2.50.

POETS AND ETCHERS. Twenty full-page etchings, by
James D. Smillie, Samuel Colman, A. F. Bellows, H. Farrer, R. Swain Gifford, illustrating poems by Longfellow, Whittier, Bryant, Aldrich, etc.
4to. $10.00. *Also limited editions on China and Japan paper.*

POOLE'S (W. F., LL.D.) An Index to Periodical Literature. 1 vol. Royal 8vo. $15.00. Sheep, $17.00. Half-morocco, $18.00.
Half-morocco, extra. Gilt top. Uncut edges, $19.00.

POPE in 1862, The Virginia Campaign of General. Vol. II.
of Papers read before the Military Historical Society of Massachusetts. 8vo.
With Maps and Plans. $3.00.

PORTER'S (Robert P.) Protection and Free Trade To-
Day: At Home and Abroad. 16mo. Paper covers, 10 cents.

PREBLE'S (Admiral George H.) History of the Flag
of the United States of America, etc. Third Revised Edition. 240 Illustrations, many of them in colors. 1 vol. Royal quarto. $7.50.

PRESTON'S (Miss H. W.) The Georgics of Vergil. 18mo. $1.

————— The Georgics of Vergil. Holiday Edition.
Four full-page Illustrations. 1 vol. Small 4to. Full gilt. $2.00.

PUTNAM'S (J. Pickering) The Open Fire-Place in all
Ages. With 300 Illustrations, 53 full-page. 12mo. $4.00.

————— Lectures on the Principles of House Drainage.
With Plates and Diagrams. 16mo. 75 cents.

QUINCY'S (Edmund) The Haunted Adjutant; and other
Stories. Edited by his son, Edmund Quincy. 1 vol. 12mo. $1.50.

————— Wensley; and other Stories. Edited by his
son, Edmund Quincy. 1 vol. 12mo. $1.50.

RACHEL'S SHARE OF THE ROAD. Vol. XVI. of
the Round-Robin Series of novels. $1.00. In paper covers, 50 cents.

REVEREND IDOL (A). A Novel. 12mo. Twelfth
edition. $1.50.

RICHARDSON'S (Abby Sage) Abelard and Heloise.
1 vol. Little-Classic size. $1.00.

————— Old Love-Letters; or, Letters of Senti-
ment. Written by persons eminent in English Literature and History.
1 vol. Little-Classic size. $1.25.

ROCKHILL'S (W. Woodville) The Life of the Buddha,
and the Early History of his Order. 1 vol. 12mo. Gilt top. $3.00.

ROLFE'S (William J.) Scott's The Lady of the Lake,
etc. See Scott.

————— The Princess, etc. See Tennyson.

ROSEMARY AND RUE. Vol. VII. of the Round-Robin
Series of novels. 16mo. $1.00. In paper covers, 50 cents.

ROUND-ROBIN SERIES (THE). A series of original
novels by the best writers. Each is complete in 1 vol. 16mo. $1.00.
Also, new popular edition, in paper covers, each, 50 cents.

A Nameless Nobleman.	A Tallahassee Girl.
A Lesson in Love.	Dorothea.
The Georgians.	The Desmond Hundred.
Patty's Perversities.	Leone.
Homoselle.	Doctor Ben.
Damen's Ghost.	Rachel's Share of the Road.
Rosemary and Rue.	Fanchette.
Madame Lucas.	His Second Campaign.

SADI'S GULISTAN. See EASTWICK.

SANBORN'S (KATE) A Year of Sunshine. Comprising
cheerful selections for every day in the year. 1 vol. 16mo. $1.00.

————— Grandma's Garden. Leaflets, with illuminated covers. $1.25.

————— Purple and Gold. Choice Poems. Leaflets,
with illuminated covers by ROSINA EMMET. $1.25.

————— Round-Table Series of Literature Lessons.
Printed separately on sheets. Twenty-five authors. Price for each author,
enclosed in envelope, 25 cents.

SANGSTER'S (MARGARET E.) Poems of the Household.
1 vol. 16mo. $1.50.

SCHIEFNER'S (PROFESSOR) Tibetan Tales. Translated
by W. R. S. RALSTON, M.A. $5.00.

SCHOPENHAUER'S (ARTHUR) The World as Will and
Idea. Translated from the German by R. B. HALDANE, M.A., and JOHN
KEMP, M.A. 3 vols. 8vo. Vol. I. $5.00.

SCOTT'S (SIR WALTER) Marmion. Holiday Edition. Over
100 new Illustrations by famous artists. Elegantly bound. Full gilt edges.
In box, $6.00. Tree-calf, or antique morocco, $10.00. Crushed levant,
with silk linings, $25.00.

————— Marmion. Tremont Edition. 1 vol. 16mo.
Beautifully illustrated. With red lines, bevelled boards, and gilt edges,
$2.50. Half-calf, $4.00. Antique morocco, flexible calf, flexible seal or
tree-calf, $6.00.

————— Marmion. Pocket Edition. 1 vol. Little-Classic
size. With thirty Illustrations. Elegantly bound, $1.00. Half-calf,
$2.25. Antique morocco, or flexible calf or seal, $3.00. Tree-calf, $3.50.

————— Marmion. Students' Edition. Edited, with
Notes and Introduction, by W. J. ROLFE. 12mo. Illustrated. 75 cents.

————— The Lady of the Lake. Holiday Edition. 1 vol.
8vo. In box. 120 Illustrations. $6.00. Tree-calf or antique morocco,
$10.00. Calf or morocco, inlaid mosaic, $12.50. Crushed levant, with
silk linings, $25.00.

————— The Lady of the Lake. Tremont Edition. 16mo.
Beautifully illustrated. Red lines. $2.50. Half-calf, $4.00. Tree-calf,
antique morocco, flexible calf or seal, $6.00.

SCOTT'S (SIR WALTER) The Lady of the Lake. Pocket
Edition. 1 vol. Little-Classic size. 30 Illustrations. $1.00. Half-calf
$2.25. Antique morocco, flexible calf, or seal, $3.00. Tree-calf, $3.50.

——————— The Lady of the Lake. Students' Edition.
Edited, with Notes and Introduction, by W. J. ROLFE. 1 vol. 12mo.
Beautifully illustrated. 75 cents.

SENSIER'S (ALFRED) Jean-François Millet: Peasant and
Painter. Translated by HELENA DE KAY. With Illustrations. $3.00.

SHALER'S (PROFESSOR N. S.) and *DAVIS'S* (WILLIAM M.)
Illustrations of the Earth's Surface. Part I. Glaciers. Copiously illustrated. Large folio. $10.00.

SHEDD'S (MRS. JULIA A.) Famous Painters and Paintings. Revised edition. With 13 Heliotypes. 1 vol. 12mo. $3.00. Half-
calf, $5.00. Tree-calf, $7.00.

——————— Famous Sculptors and Sculpture. With thirteen
Heliotype Engravings. 12mo. $3.00. Half-calf, $5.00. Tree-calf, $7.00.

——————— Raphael : His Madonnas and Holy Families.
Illustrated with 22 full-page Heliotypes. 1 vol. 4to. Full gilt. $7.50.

SHERIDAN'S (RICHARD BRINSLEY) Comedies : The
Rivals, and the School for Scandal. Edited, with Biography and Notes and
Introduction, by BRANDER MATTHEWS. Illustrated. 1 vol. 8vo. $3.00.

SHERRATT'S (R. J.) The Elements of Hand-Railing.
38 Plates. Small folio. $2.00.

SIKES'S (WIRT) British Goblins. Welsh Folk-Lore, Fairy
Mythology, and Traditions. Illustrated. 8vo. Gilt top. $4.00.

SNIDER'S (DENTON. J.) Agamemnon's Daughter. A
poem. 1 vol. Square 16mo. Fine laid paper. $1.50.

——————— A Walk in Hellas. 1 vol. 8vo. $2.50.

SPOONER'S (SAMUEL) and *CLEMENT'S* (MRS. CLARA E.)
A Biographical History of the Fine Arts. *In preparation.*

STANWOOD'S (EDWARD) A History of Presidential Elec-
tions. 1 vol. 12mo. $1.50.

STERNBERG'S (GEORGE M., M.D.) Photo-Micrographs,
and How to Make them. Illustrated by 47 Photographs of Microscopic
Objects, reproduced by the Heliotype process. 1 vol. 8vo. $3.00.

STEVENSON'S (ALEXANDER F.) The Battle of Stone
River, near Murfreesboro', Tenn., December 30, 1862, to January 3, 1863.
1 vol. 8vo. With Maps. $3.00.

STILLMAN'S (DR. J. D. B.) The Horse in Motion, as
Shown in a Series of Views by Instantaneous Photography, and Anatomical
Illustrations in Chromo, after Drawings by WILLIAM HAUN. With a Preface
by LELAND STANFORD. 1 vol. Royal quarto. Fully illustrated. $10.00.

STIRLING'S (A.) At Daybreak. A Novel. 16mo. $1.25.

STODDARD'S (JOHN L.) Red-Letter Days Abroad. 8vo.
With 130 fine Illustrations. Richly bound, full gilt edges, in box. $5.00
In tree-calf or antique morocco, $10.00. In mosaic inlaid, calf, $12.50.

STONE'S (Charles J., F.R.S.L., F.R.Hist.C.) Christianity
before Christ ; or, Prototypes of our Faith and Culture. Crown 8vo. $3.0J.

SWEETSER'S (M. F.) Artist-Biographies. With twelve
Heliotypes in each volume. 5 vols. 16mo. Cloth. Each, $1.50.

    Vol. I. Raphael, Leonardo, Angelo.
    Vol. II. Titian, Guido, Claude.
    Vol. III. Reynolds, Turner, Landseer.
    Vol. IV. Dürer, Rembrandt, Van Dyck.
    Vol. V. Angelico, Murillo, Allston.
The set, in box, 5 vols. $7.50. Half-calf, $15.00. Tree-calf, $25.00.
Flexible calf, elegant leather case, $28.00.

TALLAHASSEE GIRL (A). Vol. IX. of the Round-
Robin Series of novels. 16mo. $1.00. In paper covers, 50 cents.

TENNYSON'S (Lord) A Dream of Fair Women. Forty
Illustrations. 4to. $5.00. In morocco antique or tree-calf, $9.00.

———————— The Princess. Holiday Edition. 120 Illustrations. Rich binding. In a box. 8vo. $6.00. Morocco antique
or tree-calf, $10.00. Crushed levant, with silk linings, $25.00.

———————— The Princess. Tremont Edition. 1 vol.
16mo. Beautifully illustrated. With red lines, bevelled boards, and gilt
edges, $2.50. Half-calf, $4.00. Antique morocco, flexible calf, flexible seal
or tree-calf, $6.00.

———————— The Princess. Pocket Edition. 1 vol.
Little-Classic size. With 30 Illustrations. Elegantly bound, $1.00. Half-
calf, $2.25. Antique morocco, or flexible calf or seal, $3.00. Tree-calf, $3.50.

———————— The Princess. Students' Edition. Edited,
with Notes and Introduction, by W. J. Rolfe. 12mo. Illustrated. 75 cents.

———————— Select Poems. Students' Edition. Edited,
with Notes and Introduction, by W. J. Rolfe. Beautifully illustrated,
1 vol. 12mo. 75 cents.

THACKERAY (William M.), The Ballads of. Complete
illustrated edition. Small quarto. Handsomely bound. $1.50.

THOMAS A KEMPIS'S The Imitation of Christ. 16mo.
Red edges. 300 cuts. $1.50. Flexible calf or morocco, $4.00.
    Pocket edition. Round corners. $1.00. Flexible calf, $3.00.
    Edition de luxe. 8vo. Many full-page etchings, red ruling, etc. Full
leather binding, $9.00. In parchment covers, $5.00.

THOMPSON'S (Maurice) Songs of Fair Weather. $1.50.

TICKNOR'S AMERICAN GUIDE-BOOKS : Newly re-
vised and Augmented Editions.

    New England. With nineteen Maps and Plans. Ninth edition. 16mo. $1.50.
    The Maritime Provinces. With ten Maps and Plans. Fifth edition.
    16mo. $1.50.
    The White Mountains. With six Maps and six Panoramas. Seventh
    edition. 16mo. $1.50.
    The Middle States. With twenty-two Maps and Plans. 16mo. *Seventh*
    Edition in preparation.

TICKNOR'S COMPLETE POCKET GUIDE TO EU-
ROPE. Revised edition. With six Maps. 32mo. $1.50.

TOWLE'S (George Makepeace) England and Russia in
Central Asia. No. 1, Timely-Topics Series. 1 vol. 16mo. With Maps.
50 cents.

———— England in Egypt. No. 2, Timely-Topics Series.
1 vol. 16mo. With Maps. 50 cents.

TOWNSEND'S (Mary Ashley) Down the Bayou. A
volume of Poems. 12mo. $1.50.

TOWNSEND'S (S. Nugent) Our Indian Summer in the
Far West. With full-page Photographs of Scenes in Kansas, Colorado,
New Mexico, Texas, etc. 4to. $20.00.

UNDERWOOD'S (Francis H.) John Greenleaf Whittier.
A Biography. 1 vol. 12mo. Illustrated. $1.50.

———— Henry Wadsworth Longfellow. 12mo.
Illustrated. $1.50.

———— James Russell Lowell. A Biographical
Sketch. 1 vol. Small quarto. 6 Heliotypes. $1.50.

VIOLLET-LE-DUC'S (E. E.) Discourses on Architecture.
Vol. I. Translated by Henry Van Brunt. With 18 large Plates and 110
Woodcuts. 8vo. $5.00.

VIOLLET-LE-DUC (E. E.). *The Same.* Vol. II. With
Steel Plates, Chromos, and Woodcuts. 8vo. $5.00.

WALLACE'S (Susan E.) The Storied Sea. 1 vol. Little-
Classic size. $1.00.

WARE'S (Professor William R.) Modern Perspective.
A Treatise upon the Principles and Practice of Plane and Cylindrical Perspective. 1 vol. 12mo. With Portfolio of 27 Plates. $5.00.

WARING'S (Col. George E., Jr.) Whip and Spur.
Little-Classic size. $1.25.

———— Village Improvements and Farm Villages.
Little-Classic size. Illustrated. 75 cents.

———— The Bride of the Rhine. Two Hundred Miles
in a Mosel Row-Boat. To which is added a paper on the Latin poet
Ausonius and his poem "Mosella," by Rev. Charles T. Brooks. 1 vol.
Square 16mo. Fully illustrated. $1.50.

———— Vix. No. 1 of Waring's Horse-Stories. 10 cents.

———— Ruby. No. 2 of Waring's Horse-Stories. 10 cents.

WARNER'S (Charles Dudley) The American News-
paper. 32mo. 25 cents.

WARREN'S (Joseph H., M.D.) A Plea for the Cure of
Rupture. 12mo. In cloth, $1.25. In parchment paper covers, $1.00.

———— A Practical Treatise on Hernia. 8vo. $5.00.
Sheep. $6.50.

WEDGWOOD'S (Hensleigh) Contested Etymologies in
the Dictionary of the Rev. W. W. Skeat. 1 vol. 12mo. $2.00.

WEEKS'S (Lyman H.) Among the Azores. 1 vol. Square
16mo. With Map and 25 Illustrations. $1.50.

WELLS'S (KATE GANNETT) About People.   A volume of
Essays. Little-Classic size. $1.25.

WENDELL'S (BARRETT) The Duchess Emilia.   1 vol.
16mo. $1.00.

· *WHEELER'S* (CHARLES GARDNER) The Course of Em-
pire ; Being Outlines of the Chief Political Changes in the History of the
World. 1 vol. 8vo. With 25 colored Maps. $3.00. Half-calf, $5.50.

WHEELER'S (WILLIAM A. and CHARLES G.) Familiar
Allusions : A Handbook of Miscellaneous Information. 12mo. $3.00.
Half-calf, $5.50.

WHIST, American or Standard.   By G. W. P.   Sixth
edition. Revised and enlarged. 16mo. $1.00.

WILLIAMS'S (ALFRED M.) The Poets and Poetry of Ire-
land. With Critical Essays and Notes. 1 vol. 12mo. $2.00.

WINCKELMANN'S (JOHN) The History of Ancient Art.
Translated by Dr. G. H. LODGE. With 78 copperplate Engravings. 2 vols.
8vo. $9.00. Half-calf, $18.00. Morocco antique or tree-calf, $25.00.

WINTER'S (WILLIAM) English Rambles, and other Fugitive Pieces in Prose and Verse. 1 vol. 12mo. $1.50.

——————— Poems.   New revised edition.   1 vol.   16mo.
Cloth, $1.50. Half-calf, $3.00. Morocco antique or tree-calf, $4.00.

——————— The Trip to England.   With Illustrations by
JOSEPH JEFFERSON. 16mo. $2.00. Half-calf, $4.00. Morocco antique or
tree-calf, $5.00.

WOODS'S (REV. LEONARD) History of the Andover Theo-
logical Seminary. 1 vol. 8vo. $3.50.

MR. HOWELLS'S LATEST NOVELS.
Indian Summer. The Rise of Silas Lapham. A Woman's
Reason. A Modern Instance. Dr. Breen's Practice. A
Fearful Responsibility. Each in 1 vol. 12mo. $1.50. The 6
volumes in a neat box, $9.00.
" There has been no more rigidly artistic writing done in America since Haw-
thorne's time." — *The Critic* (N. Y.).

MR. HOWELLS'S COMEDIES. Each in 1 vol. 16mo. $1.25.
Out of the Question.   A Counterfeit Presentment.

MR. HOWELLS'S PLAYS. Each in 1 vol. 32mo. 50 cents.
The Register.   The Parlor-Car.
The Sleeping-Car.   The Elevator.

MR. HOWELLS'S POEMS. Printed on imported hand-made
paper. White parchment covers. Enlarged edition. $2.00.

THREE VILLAGES. 1 vol. Little-Classic size. $1.25.

CHOICE AUTOBIOGRAPHIES. 8 vols. 16mo. $1.25 each.

TICKNOR & COMPANY'S NEW BOOKS,

SPRING OF 1886.

The prices named below are subject to revision on publication.

ROMANCE AND REVERIE. By Edgar Fawcett.
1 vol. 12mo. Printed on fine hand-made paper, with gilt top. $2.00.
A volume of poems, by the author of " Song and Story."
" Mr. Fawcett was the man of whom Longfellow expected more than from any of the other young American authors, both as a poet and novelist." — *American Queen.*
" The *Revue des Deux Mondes* gives high praise to Mr. Fawcett's poetry, and compares his briefer lyrics to the famous ' Emaux et Camées ' of Théophile Gautier " — *Beacon.*

STORIES AND SKETCHES. By John Boyle O'Reilly, editor of the *Pilot*, author of " Moondyne," Songs, Legends, Ballads, etc. 1 vol. 12mo. $1.50.
The great popularity of the author, and the intrinsic merit and interest of his writings, will ensure a warm reception to this collection of his latest and best works.

МОРОЗЪ КРАСНЫЙ-НОСЪ (Red-Nosed Frost). Составилъ Николай Алексеевичъ Некрасовъ. Translated in the original meters from the Russian of N. A. Nekrasov.

CHRISTIAN. SYMBOLS AND STORIES OF THE SAINTS. By Clara Erskine Clement Assisted by Katherine E. Conway 1 vol. Large 12mo., with many full page illustrations. $2.50.
This is a revised version of the greater part of the author's " Hand-book of Legendary Art," — of which seventeen large editions have been exhausted. The clear and beautiful explanation of the expressive symbols by which men's minds are helped to reverent contemplation of the mysteries of revealed religion, leaves nothing to be desired. The " Stories of the Saints " will be illustrated by numerous full page engravings from the rarest and finest works of the great masters of Christian Art — prominence being given to scenes from the life of the Blessed Virgin, and pictures of the Evangelists, and the Founders and notable Saints of the Religious Orders.

MONOGRAPHS OF AMERICAN ARCHITECTURE.
No. II. The Hartford Capitol. R. M. Upjohn, Architect.
No. III. Ames Memorial Buildings, North Easton. H. H. Richardson, Architect.
Gelatine Plates (from nature), 13 x 16. Each in portfolio. $5.00.
The remarkable success of the first Monograph shows the demand existing for artistic work of this high grade ; and an equal sale may be predicted for the portfolio that illustrates the beautiful marble Gothic building of the Connecticut State Capitol. This possesses perhaps even a higher interest than the Harvard Law School, because it is a great public building, and not an appendage of an institution.
The American Architect says : " The execution of the work is all that could be asked. It would be hard to offer a more encouraging example of the kind of work to be expected in this series."

JOHN BODEWIN'S TESTIMONY. By MARY HALLOCK
FOOTE, Author of "The Led Horse Claim," &c. 1 vol. 12mo. $1.50.
"Mrs. Foote's first novel raised her to a level on which she is only to be
compared with our best women novelists. To make this comparison briefly,
Miss Woolson observes keenly, Mrs. Burnett writes charmingly, and Mrs.
Foote feels intensely." — *The Critic.*

NEXT DOOR. By CLARA LOUISE BURNHAM, Author of
"Dearly Bought," "A Sane Lunatic," &c. 1 vol. 12mo. $1.50.
One of the brightest, prettiest, and most charming tales yet offered to the
public. The scene is in Boston, the time the present; the plot exciting, the
characters lifelike, while the style is graceful and skilful.

POETS AND PROBLEMS. By GEORGE WILLIS COOKE,
Author of "Emerson; His Life, Writings and Philosophy." 1 vol. 12mo.
$2.00.
Mr. Cooke brings to his work the most inexhaustible and painstaking
patience, the most thorough devotion to the labor he has undertaken, and
the deepest mental sympathy with his subjects. His present work embraces
Tennyson, Ruskin, and Browning.

THE OLDEN-TIME SERIES. 16mo. Per vol., 50 cents.
There appears to be, from year to year, a growing popular taste for quaint
and curious reminiscences of "Ye Olden Time," and to meet this, Mr.
Henry M. Brooks has prepared a series of interesting handbooks. The
materials have been gleaned chiefly from old newspapers of Boston and
Salem, sources not easily accessible, and while not professing to be history,
the volumes will contain much material for history, so combined and
presented as to be both amusing and instructive. The titles of some of the
volumes indicate their scope and their promise of entertainment : — "Curiosities of the Old Lottery," "Days of the Spinning Wheel," "Some
Strange and Curious Punishments," "Quaint and Curious Advertisements,"
"Literary Curiosities," "New-England Sunday," etc.

*THE IMPERIAL ISLAND — ENGLAND'S CHRON-
ICLE IN STONE.* By JAMES F. HUNNEWELL. 1 vol. 8vo. Richly
illustrated. $3.50.
This admirable and impressive work is a companion to the same author's
well-known "Historical Monuments of France," and contains a vivid
record of the life of Merrie England, as exemplified by her august castles
and palaces, abbeys and cathedrals.

LIFE AND WORKS OF MRS. CLEMMER.

AN AMERICAN WOMAN'S LIFE AND WORK.
A Memorial of Mary Clemmer, by EDMUND HUDSON, with Portrait.

POEMS OF LIFE AND NATURE.

HIS TWO WIVES.

MEN, WOMEN, AND THINGS. Revised and
augmented.
The whole in four 12mo volumes, tastefully bound, forming a beautiful, uniform set of the selected works, together with the memorial
biography of this popular and lamented writer.

THE SAUNTERER.   By CHARLES GOODRICH WHITING.
1 vol. 16mo. $1.25.

A rare and choice collection of charming little essays and poems about nature, some of which have won the highest possible commendation from Stedman and other eminent critics. The author has for many years been connected with the editorial staff of "The Springfield Republican."

THE LOST NAME.   By MRS. MADELEINE VINTON DAHL-
GREN, author of "A Washington Winter," "South-sea Sketches," etc. 1 vol. 12mo. $1.50.

The remarkable success of Mrs. Dahlgren's previous portrayals of society make it certain that her forthcoming work will be full of life and purpose, and therefore sure to attract and interest.

ITALIAN POETS.   By W. D. HOWELLS.   12mo. $1.50.
Biographical and Critical Notices of the masters of Italian poetry.

A SEA CHANGE; or, Love's Stowaway.   A Comic
opera.   By W. D. HOWELLS. 1 vol. 16mo. Little-Classic size.

*THE VIRGINIA CAMPAIGN OF GENERAL POPE
IN* 1862.   Being Volume II. of Papers read before the Military Historical Society of Massachusetts. With Maps and Plans. 1 vol. 8vo. $3.00.

THE YOUNG PEOPLE'S TENNYSON.   Students'
Edition. 1 vol. 16mo. Edited, with Notes and Introduction, by W. J. Rolfe. Beautifully illustrated. 75 cents.

SELECT POEMS OF TENNYSON.   Second Part.
Students' Edition. Edited, with Notes and Introduction, by W. J. Rolfe. 1 vol. 16mo. Beautifully illustrated. 75 cents.

*SONGS AND BALLADS OF THE OLD PLANTA-
TIONS, BY UNCLE REMUS.* By JOEL CHANDLER HARRIS. 1 vol. 12mo. $1.50.

"Uncle Remus's" legends have created a strong demand for his songs, which will be eagerly welcomed.

A ROMANTIC YOUNG LADY.   By ROBERT GRANT,
author of "The Confessions of a Frivolous Girl," "An Average Man," etc. 1 vol. 12mo. $1.50.

This is the latest and one of the strongest works of the successful delineator of modern society life and manners. It will be read eagerly and enjoyably by thousands of lovers of the best fiction.

*A NEW AND ENLARGED CONCORDANCE TO
THE HOLY SCRIPTURES.* By Rev. J. B. R. WALKER.

This monumental work of patient industry and iron diligence is indispensable to all students of the Bible, to which it is the key and introduction. Many errors and omissions in the plans of the older Concordances have been avoided in this one, which also bears reference to the Revised Bible, as well as to the King-James version.

JUST PUBLISHED.

THE STORY OF MARGARET KENT. By HENRY
HAYES. 1 vol. 12mo. $1.50. 6th thousand.

A new and thrilling novel of literary life in New York, written with masterly skill. One of the most exacting of reviewers says that it will "convince and touch thoughtful and sensitive readers"; and another, a well-known novelist and poet, says: "The plot and situations are original and natural. It is out of the common run, and sparkles with life — real life — and deep feeling."

AMERICAN WHIST. By G. W. P. 1 vol. 16mo.
Sixth Edition, Revised. $1.00.

A new and fully revised and much-enlarged edition of this foremost classic, best teacher, and wisest companion as to the most enjoyable game of cards. After running through several successful editions during the past five years, this invaluable book is now to be brought out improved in many ways, and will be indispensable to all who play Whist.

CLEOPATRA. By HENRY GRÉVILLE. Original Copyright Edition, with new Portrait. 1 vol. 16mo. $1.25.

"Cleopatra" is a brilliant new novel by the author of "Dosia" and "Dosia's Daughter," who is acknowledged as foremost among the European novelists of to-day. The remarkable success that has attended Henry Gréville's previous works, foreshadows the popular demand for "Cleopatra," her latest (and in many respects, her best) novel.

EVERY-DAY RELIGION. By REV. JAMES FREEMAN
CLARKE, D.D., Author of "Self-Culture," "The Ideas of Paul," &c., &c.
1 vol. 12mo. $1.50.

An admirable group of terse, strong, and practical discourses on the religion of the home, the office, the work-shop, and the field. It tells how, amid the cares and annoyances of this workaday world, one may grow towards a noble and peaceful life. It will be an invaluable companion, an indispensable "guide, philosopher, and friend." The eminent success of JAMES FREEMAN CLARKE in works of this high class is shown by the great popularity of his "Self-Culture," which is now in its eleventh edition.

EDGE-TOOLS OF SPEECH. By MATURIN M. BALLOU,
Author of "A Treasury of Thought," "Due South," &c., &c. 1 vol.
8vo. $3.50.

"A great new work, in which are preserved the choicest expressions and opinions of the great thinkers and writers of all ages, from Confucius to Ruskin. These pungent apothegms and brilliant *memorabilia* are all carefully classified by topics; so that the choicest work of many years of patient labor in the libraries of America and Europe is condensed into perfect form and made readily available. It will be indispensable to all writers and speakers, and should be in every library" — *Traveller.*

TWO COLLEGE GIRLS. By HELEN DAWES BROWN.
1 vol. 12mo. $1.50.

One of the most important of recent books. It is a capital study of girl-students from Boston, New York, and Chicago, exemplifying the most piquant characteristics of the respective phases of civilization and social criteria of the three cities. It is suited alike to old and young, being rich in beautiful passages of tender pathos, strong, simple and vivid, and full of sustaining interest. Nothing has been published since "Little Women" that will so strike the popular taste.

LIGHT ON THE HIDDEN WAY. With an Introduction by JAMES FREEMAN CLARKE. 1 vol. 16mo. $1.00.

A remarkable and thrilling romance of immortality, illustrating by an account of personal experiences the relations between the seen and the unseen. All readers of the literature of the supernatural in books like "The Little Pilgrim," &c., will be profoundly interested in this strange record of the nearness of the spiritual and material worlds.

THE PRELATE. By ISAAC HENDERSON. 12mo. $1.50.

A story of the American colony and native society in Rome. The situations in this powerful book are among the most intense and dramatic of anything that has been offered by an American author for years.

INDIAN SUMMER. By W. D. HOWELLS, Author of "The Rise of Silas Lapham," &c. 1 vol. 12mo. $1.50.

"Mr. Howells's new story is in his pleasantest vein, full of his quiet humor clothed in the neatest expressions. It is international; the contrast of American and foreign ways runs through it, and Mr. Howells has added the contrast of the old and the new Americanism. The hero is a Western journalist, a Mugwump, much given to banter of the American sort." — *The Nation.*

A STROLL WITH KEATS. By FRANCES CLIFFORD BROWN. 1 vol. Illustrated. Square 16mo. $1.50.

One of the choicest gems of art in illustration, consisting of illuminated pages, in beautiful designs, illustrating some of the finest verses of the great English poet.

THE SPHINX'S CHILDREN AND OTHER PEO-PLE'S. By ROSE TERRY COOKE, Author of "Somebody's Neighbors," &c. 1 vol. 12mo. $1.50.

This volume of short stories, reprinted from the author's contributions to the *Atlantic, Harper's, The Galaxy*, &c., will be found like "Somebody's Neighbors," to show "that profound insight into Puritan character, and that remarkable command of Yankee dialect, in which Mrs. Cooke has but one equal, and no superior. These exquisite chronicles are full of high local color, pathos and piquancy, and their perusal is attended with alternate tears and smiles. Their narration is vigorous and spirited, sparkling in all points, and outlined with rare dramatic skill."

THE LIFE AND GENIUS OF GOETHE. The Lectures at the Concord School of Philosophy for 1885. Edited by F. B. SANBORN and W. T. HARRIS. 1 vol. 12mo. With 2 portraits. $2.00.

"A work of exceptional interest, containing fifteen of the lectures concerning Goethe which were read at the Concord School of Philosophy last summer. Prof. Hewett furnishes an account of the newly-discovered Goethe manuscripts for the introduction to the volume. Among the writers are Drs. Bartol and Hedge, Mrs. Howe, Mrs. Cheney, Mrs. Sherman of Chicago, Mr. Soldan of St. Louis, Mr. Snider of Cincinnati, Mr. Partridge of Brooklyn, N. Y., Mr. Davidson of New Jersey, Prof. White of Ithaca, N. Y., and Messrs. Emery, Harris, and Sanborn of Concord, the last named the editor." — *Traveller*

LIFE AND LETTERS OF HENRY WADSWORTH LONGFELLOW. Edited by Rev. Samuel Longfellow. 2 vols. 12mo. $6.00. With new steel engraved Portraits and many wood Engravings.

Also a limited edition de Luxe, with Proof Portraits.

The biography of the foremost American poet, written by his brother, is probably the most important work of the kind brought out in the United States for years. It is rich in domestic, personal, and family interest, anecdotes, reminiscences, and other thoroughly charming *memorabilia.*

THE

MEMORIAL HISTORY OF BOSTON,

In Four Volumes. Quarto.

With more than 500 Illustrations by famous artists and engravers, all made for this work.

Edited by JUSTIN WINSOR, LIBRARIAN OF HARVARD UNIVERSITY.

Among the contributors are : —

Gov. JOHN D. LONG,	Dr. O. W. HOLMES,
Hon. CHARLES FRANCIS ADAMS,	JOHN G. WHITTIER,
Rev. PHILLIPS BROOKS, D D.,	Rev. J. F. CLARKE, D.D.,
Rev. E. E. HALE, D.D.,	Rev. A. P. PEABODY, D.D.,
Hon. ROBERT C. WINTHROP,	Col. T. W. HIGGINSON,
Hon. J. HAMMOND TRUMBULL,	Professor ASA GRAY,
Admiral G. H. PREBLE,	Gen. F. W. PALFREY,

HENRY CABOT LODGE.

VOLUME I. treats of the Geology, Fauna, and Flora; the Voyages and Maps of the Northmen, Italians, Captain John Smith, and the Plymouth Settlers; the Massachusetts Company, Puritanism, and the Aborigines; the Literature, Life, and Chief Families of the Colonial Period.

VOL. II. treats of the Royal Governors; French and Indian Wars; Witches and Pirates; The Religion, Literature, Customs, and Chief Families of the Provincial Period.

VOL. III. treats of the Revolutionary Period and the Conflict around Boston; and the Statesmen, Sailors, and Soldiers, the Topography, Literature, and Life of Boston during that time; and also of the Last Hundred Years' History, the War of 1812, Abolitionism, and the Press.

VOL. IV. treats of the Social Life, Topography, and Landmarks, Industries, Commerce, Railroads, and Financial History of this Century in Boston; with Monographic Chapters on Boston's Libraries, Women, Science, Art, Music, Philosophy, Architecture, Charities, etc.

*** *Sold by subscription only. Send for a Prospectus to the Publishers,*

TICKNOR AND COMPANY, Boston.

THE CHOICEST EDITIONS

OF THE

FIVE GREAT MODERN POEMS.

——◆——

Drawn and engraved under the care of A. V. S. ANTHONY. Each in one volume, 8vo, elegantly bound, with full gilt edges, in a neat box. Each poem, in cloth, $6.00 ; in tree calf, or antique morocco, $10.00; in crushed levant, extra, with silk linings, $25.00. Copiously illustrated after drawings by Thomas Moran, E. H. Garrett, Harry Fenn, A. B. Frost, and other distinguished artists.

CHILDE HAROLD.

The choicest gift-book of 1885-1886. With nearly 100 noble Illustrations, of great artistic value and beauty, representing the splendid scenery and architecture of the Rhine, Greece, Italy, etc.

THE PRINCESS.

The most famous poem of ALFRED, LORD TENNYSON. With 120 new and beautiful Illustrations.

" The most superb book of the season. The exquisite binding makes a fit casket for Tennyson's enchanting ' Princess.' " — *Hartford Journal.*

THE LADY OF THE LAKE.

A superb fine-art edition, with 120 Illustrations. The choicest edition of Scott's wonderful poem of Scottish chivalry.

" On page after page are seen the great dome of Ben-an rising in mid-air, huge Ben-venue throwing his shadowed masses upon the lakes, and the long heights of Ben Lomond hemming the horizon." — *Atlantic Monthly.*

LUCILE.

By OWEN MEREDITH. With 160 Illustrations.

The high peaks of the Pyrenees, the golden valleys of the Rhineland, and the battle-swept heights of the Crimea.

" This new edition is simply perfect — paper, type, printing, and especially the illustrations, — a most charming Christmas gift." — *American Literary Churchman.*

MARMION.

With more than 100 Illustrations, and Borders.

" Wild Scottish beauty. Never had a poem of stately and immortal beauty a more fitting setting." — *Chicago Inter-Ocean.*

——◆——

For Sale by Booksellers. Sent, postpaid, on receipt of price, by the Publishers,

TICKNOR AND COMPANY, Boston.

THE
AMERICAN ARCHITECT
AND BUILDING NEWS.
An Illustrated Weekly Journal of Architecture and the Building Trades.

Each number is accompanied by six fine quarto illustrations, while illustrative cuts are liberally used in the text. Although the paper addresses itself primarily to architects and builders, by its discussions upon matters of interest common to those engaged in building pursuits, it is the object of the editors to make it acceptable and necessary to that large portion of the educated classes who are interested in and appreciate the importance of good architectural surroundings, to civil and sanitary engineers, draughtsmen, antiquaries, craftsmen of all kinds, and all intelligent readers.

As an indication of the feeling with which this journal is regarded by the profession, we quote the following extract from a report of a committee of the American Institute of Architects upon " American Architectural Journals ": —

"At Boston, Mass., is issued the AMERICAN ARCHITECT AND BUILDING NEWS, a weekly of the first class, and, it must be acknowledged, the only journal in this country that can compare favorably with the great London architectural publications. It is very liberally illustrated with full-page lithographic impressions of the latest designs of our most noted architects, and with occasional views of celebrated European buildings. Once a month a fine gelatine print is issued in a special edition. Its editorial department is conducted in a scholarly, courteous, and, at the same time, independent tone, and its selections made with excellent judgment. It is the accepted exemplar of American architectural practice, and is found in the office of almost every architect in the Union." — *April* 15, 1885.

Subscription Prices. (In Advance.)

REGULAR EDITION. — $6.00 per year; $3.50 per half year.

GELATINE EDITION (the same as the regular edition, but including 12 or more Gelatine Prints). — $7.00 per year; $4.00 per half year.

IMPERIAL EDITION (the same as the regular edition, but including 40 Gelatine Prints, and 36 additional double-page Photo-Lithographic Prints). — $10.00 year; $6.00 per half year.

MONTHLY EDITION (identical with the first weekly issue for each month, but containing no Gelatine Prints). — $1.75 per year; $1.00 per half year.

Bound volumes for 1876, 1877, 1878, 1879, 1880, 1881, $10.50; 1882, 1883, 1884, and 1885, $9.00 each.

Bound volume (Gelatine edition) for 1885, $10.00.

Specimen numbers and advertising rates furnished on application to the publishers,

TICKNOR AND COMPANY,
211 TREMONT STREET, BOSTON, MASS.

CPSIA information can be obtained at www.ICGtesting.com
Printed in the USA
BVOW021003240513

321595BV0001 B/333/P